Trial of Sir Robert T. Wilson, John H. Hutchinson, and Michael Bruce, for Assisting in The Escape of M. Lavalette. With a Brief Memoir of Sir R.T. Wilson

William Galloway

Trial of Sir Robert T. Wilson, John H. Hutchinson, and Michael Bruce, for Assisting in The Escape of M. Lavalette. With a Brief Memoir of Sir R.T. Wilson

The Making of Modern Law collection of legal archives constitutes a genuine revolution in historical legal research because it opens up a wealth of rare and previously inaccessible sources in legal, constitutional, administrative, political, cultural, intellectual, and social history. This unique collection consists of three extensive archives that provide insight into more than 300 years of American and British history. These collections include:

Legal Treatises, 1800-1926: over 20,000 legal treatises provide a comprehensive collection in legal history, business and economics, politics and government.

Trials, 1600-1926: nearly 10,000 titles reveal the drama of famous, infamous, and obscure courtroom cases in America and the British Empire across three centuries.

Primary Sources, 1620-1926: includes reports, statutes and regulations in American history, including early state codes, municipal ordinances, constitutional conventions and compilations, and law dictionaries.

These archives provide a unique research tool for tracking the development of our modern legal system and how it has affected our culture, government, business – nearly every aspect of our everyday life. For the first time, these high-quality digital scans of original works are available via print-on-demand, making them readily accessible to libraries, students, independent scholars, and readers of all ages.

The BiblioLife Network

This project was made possible in part by the BiblioLife Network (BLN), a project aimed at addressing some of the huge challenges facing book preservationists around the world. The BLN includes libraries, library networks, archives, subject matter experts, online communities and library service providers. We believe every book ever published should be available as a high-quality print reproduction; printed on-demand anywhere in the world. This insures the ongoing accessibility of the content and helps generate sustainable revenue for the libraries and organizations that work to preserve these important materials.

The following book is in the "public domain" and represents an authentic reproduction of the text as printed by the original publisher. While we have attempted to accurately maintain the integrity of the original work, there are sometimes problems with the original work or the micro-film from which the books were digitized. This can result in minor errors in reproduction. Possible imperfections include missing and blurred pages, poor pictures, markings and other reproduction issues beyond our control. Because this work is culturally important, we have made it available as part of our commitment to protecting, preserving, and promoting the world's literature.

GUIDE TO FOLD-OUTS MAPS and OVERSIZED IMAGES

The book you are reading was digitized from microfilm captured over the past thirty to forty years. Years after the creation of the original microfilm, the book was converted to digital files and made available in an online database.

In an online database, page images do not need to conform to the size restrictions found in a printed book. When converting these images back into a printed bound book, the page sizes are standardized in ways that maintain the detail of the original. For large images, such as fold-out maps, the original page image is split into two or more pages

Guidelines used to determine how to split the page image follows:

• Some images are split vertically; large images require vertical and horizontal splits.
• For horizontal splits, the content is split left to right.
• For vertical splits, the content is split from top to bottom.
• For both vertical and horizontal splits, the image is processed from top left to bottom right.

SIR ROBERT THOMAS WILSON

Edinburgh Published by J.Dick No 142 High Street.

TRIAL

OF

SIR ROBERT T. WILSON, JOHN H. HUTCHIN-

SON, and MICHAEL BRUCE,

FOR

ASSISTING IN THE ESCAPE

OF

M. LAVALETTE.

WITH

A BRIEF MEMOIR OF

SIR R. T. WILSON.

12

EDINBURGH:

Printed for J. DICK, 142, HIGH STREET.

By A. & J. Aikman.

Rec. Feb. 8, 1899.

TRIAL

OF

SIR ROBERT T. WILSON, &c.

WITH A

BRIEF MEMOIR OF HIS LIFE.

———————

THE particulars of the Life of this gentleman, the inveterate enemy of Bonaparte, were always interesting. His late arrest, confinement, trial, and condemnation for assisting in the escape of Lavalette have made them more so. It is proposed, therefore, in the following tract to give a rapid sketch of them, and to proceed to the more important circumstances attending his late persecution, into which we shall introduce the examinations of his accomplices in this transaction.

Sir Robert Thomas Wilson is the son of Benjamin Wilson, F.R.S., a painter, and was born in London in 1777. His father was draughtsman to the Board of Ordnance; and possessed, considerable literary abilities which he exercised in writing upon subjects connected with Natural Philosophy. The first rudiments of education he was taught at Westminster; he completed his studies at Winchester at the early age of eleven, when he lost his father.

At this period it apppears that his mind was fired with a desire for military fame, no doubt from the accounts he had read in history of the heroic deeds of our ancestors; and he resolved to join the army. This he was enabled to do as an officer, from the patrimony left him.

Having joined the army in Holland under the Duke of York in 1793, he was introduced by his brother-in-law (Lieut.-Col. Boswell of the Coldstream Guards,) to his Royal Highness; and very soon acquired, what his youthful mind aimed at. Being instrumental in saving the life of the Emperor Francis II. at Landrecies in the year 1794, when his Majesty having ventured too far from his camp with a feeble escort, was in danger of being cut off; Sir Robert, with a small handful of men, so struck the enemy with dread, as to cause their retreat, from the idea that he had a larger force to support him. The Emperor of Germany, sensible of his merit, rewarded him at this time with a medal struck on purpose; and afterwards so far relaxed the regulations of the order of Maria Theresa, as to confer upon him the cross of that order.

Sir Robert remained on the continent while the British army under the Duke of York were able to effect any thing, and afterwards was employed in Ireland; thereafter he was commanded once more to place himself under the orders of his Royal Highness in the ill-fated expedition to Holland. By this time he was promoted to the rank of Major in Hompesch's Dragoons, and accompanied it to Egypt in the expedition under the late Sir Ralph Abercromby. The narrative of this campaign we cannot repeat; it did immortal honour to our country, and no man did more to render the conduct of Bonaparte infamous than Sir Robert Wilson. His history of that campaign has long been before the public; and in his trial he has not denied a syllable advanced by him therein; we therefore claim for him that confidence as a historian which he is entitled to as a warrior.

After the expedition to Egypt Sir Robert returned to England, and during the peace of Amiens occupied his leisure in preparing his celebrated account of that campaign, which brought upon him the personal hatred of Bonaparte, to which he answered by an appeal to the French, and to Bonaparte himself, for the truth of his statements, daring the contradiction of them.

On the breaking out of the war in 1803, nothing of a military nature took place with France, (except the re-occupation of the West India colonies we had prematurely given up,) till the unwarrantable attack of Bonaparte on Spain. The assistance we rendered to the patriots, determined to resist the authority of an unprincipled invader, in behalf of an ungrateful Sovereign, is well known. Sir Robert Wilson, of course, served with his regiment. On every occasion where he was employed, he evinced the same fearless courage and disregard of personal safety that had marked his previous career, and often received from his commander testimonies to that effect. He had the misfortune, however, to be taken prisoner by Marshal Ney, (from whom he received the kindest treatment, and which accounts for the interest he took in the fate of that individual,) and after being exchanged, he offered his services in another quarter, and was in consequence appointed to a post of confidence—viz. to accompany the armies of the Emperor Alexander when Bonaparte made as unwarrantable an attack on Russia. Sir Robert, by his counsels, contributed greatly to the success of our Allies in the North, and was present at every battle of consequence which was fought, till the French were driven into their own territories; and for which he received the marked approbation of the Allied Monarchs.

The irruption of Bonaparte, after his exile to Elba, banished the hope of a lasting peace; and accordingly all Europe, hastened to the combat. It is unnecessary here to detail the particulars of the short but momentous campaign of 1815—we only notice that the name of Sir Robert Wilson does not appear prominent in its annals. The first notice we have of his appearance again on the public stage, is connected with the particular part which he took in the escape of Lavalette, and which forms the contents of the present pamphlet.

Lavalette it is well known was the Director General of the Posts under Bonaparte during his reign, and being suffered to remain in France during the peace, he was placed again in the same situation (or as the pleadings stated, had assumed a part to which he had no right). In this situation he was enabled to afford great facility to the operations of Bonaparte, in forwarding his proclamations, &c. to every part of France, and keeping back the addresses, &c. of Louis XVIII. which had been left after the King's flight from Paris, for general circulation. For this crime he was doomed to suffer death; and was to have been executed on the 21st December; but the evening previous, through the exemplary courage and artifice of his Wife (only 27 years of age) he escaped the vigilance of his gaolers, and having found a temporary concealment in the house of one of Sir Robert's friends, he was by them escorted out of the French territories, and is now safe, nobody knows where.

Sir Robert and his co-adjutors remained in Paris, free from any suspicion that the French Government had any knowledge of their concern in this matter, till the 13th of January last, when they were arrested in their beds, and have since undergone a most rigorous confinement; debarred for the greater part of the time, from any communication with their relations, or the means of consulting with legal advisers. Their trial has at length come on, and from the publicity given to the anterior proceedings—the acts of indictment, &c., we may presume the rank of the individuals concerned, rendered such conduct on the part of the French Government indispensably necessary. They were found guilty on their own confession, but received the mildest sentence the law admitted of—*Three months imprisonment.* The goaler who assisted in the escape, received the highest, *Two years imprisonment.* We now proceed to a detail of the judicial proceedings; omitting all which preceded the publication of the following :—

ARRET

Or Bill of Indictment presented by the Chamber of Accusation at Paris against Sir Robert Wilson, John Hely Hutchinson, and Michael Bruce.

On the 20th of December, 1815, about two o'clock in the afternoon, Emilie Louise de Beauharnois (femme) Lavalette, availing herself of the permission that had been given her to communicate with Marie Chamans de Lavalette, her husband, condemned to death for the crime of high treason, repaired in a sedan chair to the Conciergerie at the Palace of Justice. The chairmen were Joseph Guerin, alias Marengo, and one Brigant. Having arrived near the grate of the Conciergerie, Lavalette, the wife, alighted from the chair, and was introduced into the prison. Benoit Bonneville, her domestic, who had accompanied her, remained in the first chamber, called the Avant-greffe. During the course of this visit, Lavalette sent for his daughter, aged 13, who came, accompanied by Anne Marguerite Dutoit, a female attached to her service, and aged 60. Jean Baptiste Roquette de Kerguidec, sen. head gaoler of the House of Justice, permitted her to enter, although she was not furnished with permission to that effect.

About five o'clock in the evening Lavalette sat down to dine with his wife, his daughter, and the widow Dutoit. They were waited upon by Jacques Merle, a turnkey of the prison, particularly charged with the guard of Lavalette, who nevertheless paid him a recompense, because he employed him as a domestic.

After dinner Merle went for the coffee, which he brought, and he was requested not to come in again until he was rung for. About 7 o'clock the bell was accordingly rung, to desire Merle to tell the chairmen to be in immediate readiness, because Lavalette, the wife, was about to depart; but Lavalette, as it appears, had turned to account the time during which he had been without a keeper; had put on some of his wife's clothing, and covered his head with her bonnet and feathers; having put on a tucker and gloves, he soon after came out of the prison, with the aid of this disguise, holding his daughter by the hand, and leaning on the widow Dutoit; and it is difficult to suppose that Merle did not perceive the disguise. In order the better to deceive the vigilance of the gaoler and the other keepers, Lavalette concealed his face with a handkerchief, as if stifling his sobs, and drying up his tears.

During this time Bonneville had made himself secure of Guerin, alias Marengo, and had procured another chairman to replace Brigant, who had rejected the offer made to him. The sedan chair was then ready, Lavalette entered it, the chairmen set off, Bonneville, the widow Dutoit, and Lavalette, the daughter, following it to the end of the rue de la Barilliere, where Lavalette having arrived, left the chair, and took to flight, his daughter taking his place in it.

In the mean time the escape was not yet known in the prison, when the gaoler, Roquette, sen. entered Lavalette's chamber; he saw no one there, but he heard something stirring behind a folding screen; he went out, and returned shortly after. Having then called without receiving an answer, and feeling alarmed, he advanced towards the screen, and recognising Lavalette's wife, he immediately exclaimed; " Ah Madame, you have deceived me ;" and wished to go out to give the alarm; but it would appear that the woman, Lavalette, made some efforts to detain him. At last he got out of the Chamber, and immediately set off in pursuit of the sedan chair, which was come up with at a short distance, but no one was found in it but Lavalette, the daughter. Merle, who had received orders from Roquette, jun. to run up the rue de la Barilliere, in order to overtake, if possible, the escaped prisoner, had, on the contrary, returned to the Conciergerie, under the pretence of satisfying himself as to the reality of Lavalette's escape, and of visiting the chamber. Merle had also, at the moment of Lavalette's escape, taken to the tavern one Bodiseau, whose superinspection might have proved fatal to the success of the plan.

All these facts gave occasion to a criminal inquiry against the authors or presumed accomplices of the escape. Lavalette, the wife, being interrogated at the very moment of the event and since, has indeed persisted in declaring that she alone had conceived and executed the project; but the inquiry did not in this respect produce any direct and positive charge that could enable us to place any confidence in her declarations.

It appeared, on the contrary, to result, that Lavalette the wife wou'd not, as well as her daughter and the widow Dutoit, have taken any active part in this project, but that Lavalette would have conceived and executed, without being aided by them, his plan of escape; and that he would not have obtained from these three females any thing but a passive obedience, which their mutual relations render probable. As to Benoit Bonneville, he appears to have knowingly favoured the escape of his master, (which his situation seems to have demanded,) and to have even actively co-operated in procuring for him two chair men who could be depended upon, and by attempting to seduce the man Brigant by the offer of 25 louis. Joseph Guerin alias Marengo, does not appear exempt from active participation in the escape: he had joined his entreaties to those of Bonneville, in order to persuade Brigant to accept the offers which were made to the latter. As to the second chairman, named Chossy, no trace has appeared against him of his having knowingly participated in the escape, and he has been placed out of prosecution since the commencement of the process. The turnkey Merle, has not invalidated by his answers the charges which arose against him of having favoured, by connivance, the escape, and which result from the facts above stated. In fine, Roquette, sen. the gaoler, has not exculpated himself from the offence imputed to him, of having, by his negligence, facilitated the escape of the convict entrusted to his keeping.

The criminal inquiry, relative to the above named persons implicated had terminated, and proceedings were about to be held upon it, when an unexpected event, which appeared to be the consequence of Lavalette's escape, and had the closest connexion with the first fact, reached the ears of justice, and necessitated new inquires.

Lavalette, escaped from the Conciegerie, was still not sheltered from danger; he was still not enabled to leave Paris; and the very active searches which were made there could not have failed speedily to discover him. In order to escape from his sentence, he had no other means but that of getting out of France at all hazards; but this was perilous, because a discription of him had been sent to all the authorities, and to the gendarmerie; nevertheless it was soon learned that this convict had succeeded in getting from Paris, and even in passing the frontiers, of France; and those persons who had provided him with the means did not remain long unknown. A letter written by Sir Robert Wilson, an Englishman, a Major-General not in active service, under date of the 11th of January 1816, containing the most circumstantial details of Lavalette's escape from France, confirmed the suspicions which were excited in this respect, against the said Wilson, and also against John Hely Hutchinson and Michael Bruce. It made known the part which each of them had taken in the concealment of Lavalette and in facilitating his escape out of France.

In consequence a criminal inquiry was directed against them. On this inquiry, it appeared that, from the 1st day of January, Wilson, and Bruce, being acquainted with the fact that Lavalette was still at Paris, had formed the project of rescuing him from justice; that they had communicated this project to Hutchinson, who had joined in it ; that, in fact, on the 6th of January they met at the house of the latter, and concerted and agreed with Lavalette upon the means which it would be necessary to employ to secure the escape of this convict ; that Bruce and Hutchinson employed themselves in directing the preparation of the dress necessary to facilitate the flight of Lavalette ; that Hutchinson concealed him at his lodging on the night from the 7th to the 8th : that the following day he accompanied on horseback the cabriolet in which Wilson and Lavalette rode ; that at last the said Wilson did not quit Lavalette till after having conducted him beyond France, and having facilitated to him the means of surmounting all the obstacles which might stop him by the way. In a part of Wilson's correspondence which has reached the knowledge of justice, passages have been remarked, in which the accused, and those with whom he corresponds in England, in professing principles the most dangerous and most opposite to every kind of social order, manifested great hatred against the Government actually existing in France, and appeared to invoke by their prayers, events that might disturb its existing order, and weaken its force of stability. Expressions might be inserted, contained in these letters, to show that the partisans of these frightful doctrines, being sworn enemies of all wise and regular governments, were not far from plotting their ruin ; in consequence of this, in the inquiry which has taken place regarding Wilson and his accomplices, it has been attempted to be ascertained, if the fact which has been imputed to him, relative to the concealment and the escape of Lavalette, be connected with a plot formed by them against the internal security of the kingdom, and, if they had not for their object to produce a political commotion that might shake or even overturn the government ; but the charges which have resulted from the documents and the inquiry, however serious the character they assume, do not appear sufficient to warrant, in the terms of the law against the accused, an indictment for an attempt or a plot to overthrow the government.— The correspondence of Wilson did not present on his side a concerted and fixed resolution of acting in conformity with the frightful principles which he professes ; and Bruce and Hutchinson were besides strangers to that correspondence. Nevertheless the inquiry being terminated, and the proceedings being annexed to it in due order, the tribunal of first instance in Paris, by an ordinance, that issued from it on the second of the present month, decided on the whole of the procedure.

It charged Wilson, 1st, with a plot directed generally against the political system of Europe, and having for its particular object to destroy or change the French government, to excite the inhabitants to take up arms against the King's authority; 2d, with having endeavoured to attain the execution of this plot by seeking to snatch from the pursuit of justice, by address or by violence, individuals comprehended in the 1st article of the ordinance of the 24th of July, 1815, and principally by concerting, settling, and consummating the escape and concealment of Lavalette, condemned for the crime of high treason. Hutchinson and Bruce were charged with being accomplices of Wilson, by knowingly aiding and assisting the latter in the acts which prepared, facilitated, and consummated the same plot, and with having co-operated in its execution—videlicet, Bruce by concerting with Wilson the flight of Lavalette, and furnishing him with the means; and Hutchinson by concealing Lavalette, and accompanying him as far as Compeigne.

With regard to the individuals charged with having facilitated the escape of Lavalette from the prison of Conciergerie, the same ordinance charged Merle with having, by connivance with Lavalette, of whom he was the keeper, facilitated the escape of that convict; Roquette de Kerguidec the keeper, the widow Dutoit, Bonneville, and Guerin, with having facilitated the escape of Lavalette, the first by his negligence, and the others by their voluntary co-operation.

With regard to Lavalette the wife, considering that there did not exist against her sufficient proofs of a criminal co-operation in the escape of her husband, it was declared that there was no ground for prosecution against her at present.

The Court, after having deliberated as to what respects Wilson, Hutchinson, and Bruce, considering that there do not result from the documents and preliminary investigation sufficient charges against them of having, towards the close of 1815, and in January 1816, formed or executed a plot having for its object to destroy or alter the French Government, or to excite the citizens to take up arms against the royal authority, nor of having been accomplices in the said crimes, declares that there is no ground for accusation against the said Wilson, Hutchinson, and Bruce, in respect of the said facts of attempt and plot.

As far as respects Jacques Merle, considering that, from the preliminary investigation, the charge results against him of having, on the 20th of December, 1815, in connivance with Lavalette, condemned to capital punishment, and to the keeping of whom he was specially appointed, facilitated the escape from prison of the said Lavalette:

As far as respects Jean Baptiste Roquette de Kerguidec the elder, considering that there results from the inquiry a sufficient charge against him of having, on the 20th of December, 1815, through negligence, facilitated the escape of Lavalette, condemned to a capital punishment, and who was committed to his care in quality of chief gaoler of the prison :

As far as respects Benoit Bonneville, and Joseph Guerin, alias Marengo, considering that there results from the documents a sufficient charge against them, of having on the 20th December, 1815, facilitated the escape of Lavalette, condemned to a capital punishment, by procuring for the condemned the means of effecting his escape; and also as respects Wilson, Hutchinson, and Bruce, considering that there results from the documents a sufficient charge against them of being, in the month of January 1816, accessory to the concealment of Lavalette, knowing that he was condemned to a capital punishment, and of having facilitated the completion of his escape.

These crimes and offences being provided against by the articles 59, 61, 240, and 241 of the penal code, the Court orders the indictment of Jacques Merle, and commits him to the Court of Assize of the department of the Seine, to be tried conformably to law; and considering their connexion, and the third article of the civil code, which obliges all those who reside in France to conform in matters of police and public safety to the laws of the kingdom, commits to the same Court of Assize the aforesaid Roquette the elder, Bonneville, Guerin, Wilson, Hutchinson, and Bruce, in a state of arrest, to be tried for the offences imputed to them by the same process. As far as respects Emilie Louise Beauharnois the wife of Lavalette, and Anne Marguerite Boyeldieu, the widow of Dutoit, considering that there does not result from the documents and the inquiry, a sufficient charge against them of having lent criminal assistance to the escape of Lavalette, or of having facilitated the said escape; and that passive obedience to which they were reduced by their quality and their situation with respect to Lavalette, cannot be considered as a voluntary and active participation in the effected escape of the condemned : Decreeing that there is no ground for prosecuting the aforesaid wife of Lavalette and widow Dutoit, makes absolute the liberty granted conditionally to the said wife of Lavalette in the course of the proceedings, and orders that Marguerite Boyeldieu shall be immediately set at liberty, if she is not confined for any other cause.

FINAL ACT OF ACCUSATION AGAINST SIR ROBERT WIL- SON AND MESSRS. BRUCE AND HUTCHINSON.

MARIE CHAMONS LAVALETTE had been, on the 22d of November last, capitally convicted of the crime of high treason, by decree of the Court of Assize for the Department of the Seine. Against this decree he has appealed; but his appeal being rejected by the Court, the sentence pronounced upon him was to have been carried into effect on Thursday, December 21.

The strictest orders had been given by the Police that the condemned man should be guarded in the prison wherein he was confined, called the Conciergerie, with all the usual precautions; and since the rejection of the appeal, the Prefect of Police had ordered Jean Baptiste de Ker- guisek, the registering keeper of the prisons to redouble his vigilance; adding, that if any one should ask to communicate with Lavalette, and should even bring an order for that purpose signed with his (the Pre- fect's hand), still the keeper should pay no attention to it, as no person was to see the Prisoner without the order of the Attorney-Ge- neral.

Lavalette, being informed by the keeper of these new orders, im- mediately wrote to the Attorney-General, begging that he might be permitted to see his wife, and a few other persons, whose names he mentioned. The Attorney-General felt unwilling to refuse this re- quest; but, in giving his assent, he particularly directed that the persons indicated should only see Lavalette in succession—one after the other.

Nevertheless, on the 20th of December, the eve of the day fixed for carrying the sentence into effect, about half-past three in the after- noon, Lavalette's wife and daughter, accompanied by the widow Du- toit, who is 70 years old, and attached to the service of Mademoiselle Lavalette, were introduced at the same time by the gaoler, Roquette, into Lavalette's chamber, though the name of neither Mademoiselle Lavalette, nor that of the widow Dutoit, was inserted in the list ap- proved by the Attorney-General.

Madame Lavalette was carried to the Conciergerie in a chair borne by one Guerin, called Marengo, her ordinary chairman, and by one Brigant, a man selected for that day's service by Guerin, in the room of one Laporte, who usually performed this service with him, but who happened at this time to be ill. The chairman generally had conveyed Madame Lavalette into the court-yard of the Conciergerie, but on the 20th of December she got out in the court-yard of the palace, and walk-

B

ed on foot towards the grate of the Conciergerie; Betoit Bonneville, or valet, having told the chairmen to stop, and Madame found herself sufficiently strong to walk the rest of the way. They accordingly turned the chair towards the Palace of Justice but out of it was taken a cushion, covered with green taffety, and a pretty large package of an irregular form which seemed to contain bottles of wine. This package, as well as the cushion, and a work-bag which Madame Lavalette carried, were received in to the prison, and taken into Lavalette's chamber, without undergoing the previous examination which the regulations of the police respecting prisons always require in similar cases.

Madame Lavalette, on arriving at the Conciergerie, was clothed in a furred riding-coat of red Merino, and had upon her head a black hat, with various coloured feathers. She entered her husband's apartment, with her daughter and the widow Dutoit. The valet-de-chambre, Benoit, remained in the first apartment called the avant-greffe. He was seen near the fire-place during more than two hours. The chairmen had been received into the corps de garde of gendarmerie.

At five o'clock Jacques Eberle, one of the wicket-keepers of the Conciergerie, who had been specially appointed by the keeper of the prison to the guard and service of Lavalette, took his dinner to him, of which Madame and Mademoiselle Lavalette and the widow Dutoit partook.

After dinner, which lasted an hour, Eberle served up coffee, which he fetched from the coffee-house of the palace, and left Lavalette's apartment with orders not to return till he was rung for. Roquette, the son, maintains, on the contrary, that, on quitting the chamber of Lavalette, he said that he had received orders not to wait till he was summoned into the apartment.

However, Benoit, who was in the secret of what was intended, and who saw the hour of execution approach, had left the avant-greffe to assure himself of the chairmen. He found them at the corps-de-garde, and invited them to come and drink with him. Guerin immediately acceded, but Brigant would not stir. " Come along, comrade," said Benoit to him ; " you need not take too much." Brigant suffered himself to be persuaded. Benoit, by way of trying them, says, " Comrade, there are five and twenty louis to be gained ; you will be a little heavily loaded, and it will be necessary to go a little quick ; but you have only ten steps to make." " It is Monsieur Lavalette himself, then, that we are going to take," replies Brigant. " You have nothing to do with that : only do what you are asked." Brigant rejects the proposition, which Benoit urges, and repeats to him several times, " You are but half a man." Guerin, the other chairman, joined his entreaties, and said to Brigant, " What does it signify to you, since Monsieur assures you that there is nothing to fear !" Brigant wished to know exactly whom he had to carry. Benoit and Guerin constantly repeat that it was indifferent to him, since he had nothing to fear, and that one ought to make a little money when one could. At length, Brigant being hard pressed, and beginning to think of what advantage it would be to him and his family to yield, threw down the chair-staff, which Guerin had put into his hand, and, without entering the wine-shop, ran home as fast as he could to tell his wife what had happened.

Guerin, without losing a moment, cast his eyes upon a coalheaver, who happened to be drinking with two of his comrades at the same place. He proposed to him to take the staff of the chair. Benoit seconded him, and off they immediately go. It was now seven o'clock. Being arrived at the Court of the Palace, at the foot of the staircase which leads to the Conciergerie, they found the chair, with the door open towards the gate of the prison. Chapy (that was the name of the coalheaver who had taken Brigant's place) saw no one enter, the back part being assigned to him ; and Guerin, taking the lead, turned towards the grate of the Palace, and, after having passed it, took to the right, and followed the street of La Barillerie.

While Benoit and Guerin were employed, as has been stated, without, a scene of a different kind took place within the Conciergerie. A short time after coffee, and towards seven o'clock, the bell rang from Lavalette's chamber, intimating to the keep r that his prisoner wanted somebody.—Roquette, the father, was at that moment near the fire-place with Eberle, to whom he immediately gave orders to go into Lavalette's chamber. He hears the keeper of the wicket open the door which leads to that chamber, and, as he advanced to know what Lavalette wanted, he sees three persons dressed in female attire, who were followed by Eberle, and who came in front of him in the avant-greffe. The person whom he took for Madame Lavalette was dressed in a black petticoat, with a furred gown of red Merino : she had white gloves and a woman's neck-kerchief on, a black hat with feathers of different colours : in a word, she was exactly in the same dress as that in which Madame Lavalette was first introduced to the apartment of her husband. A white handkerchief covered the face of this person, who had the appearance of sobbing ; Mademoiselle Lavalette, who walked by the side, uttered the most lamentable cries. Every thing in that romantic scene presented the spectacle of a family given up to the feelings of a last adieu. The keeper melted, and deceived by the disguise, and scanty light of two lamps, had not the power, as he says, to take away the handkerchief, which concealed the features of the disguised person; and, having neglected to perform this painful but necessary duty, he presented his hand to the person, (as he had been used to do to Madame Lavalette), whom he conducted along with two persons to the last wicket. Eberle then stepped forward, and to tell Benoit, who arrived with the chairmen. Lavalette, under the habit of his wife, was already in the chair, which was immediately carried forward, followed by Benoit, by Madame Lavalette, and the widow Dutoit. Eberle, having at this moment perceived another wicket-keeper, took him away to drink, saying at the same time, " It is something singular that those three persons never spoke a word to me."

The chair and its suite went, according to the direction of Benoit, of Guerin, and Mademoiselle Lavalette, to the middle of the street la Barillerie ; and, according to Chapy's account, whose evidence is not to be suspected, as far as the quay des Orfevres, three or four houses beyond the street of St. Anne, where the chairmen were stopped by order of Benoit. The chair was opened, Lavalette came out, and disappeared, and was immediately succeeded in his place by Mademoiselle Lavalette. Benoit told the chairmen to turn towards the Abbaye aux Bois. In the meantime the keeper Roquette enters for the first time the chamber of Lavalette, where he sees no one, but hears somebody stirring behind the screen. He returns a second time, and calls ; no one answers. He begins to fear some mischief, advances beyond the screen, and there recognising Madame Lavalette, cries out, " Ah ! Madame you have deceived me." He wishes to run out, in order to give the alarm. Madame Lavalette catches hold of him by the coat sleeve—" Stay, Monsieur Roquette, stay." " No, Madame, this is not to be borne." A struggle ensues ; the coat is torn ! Roquette rushes out, calling for help, and informs his son of the escape of the prisoner.

Roquette the son, darts from the Conciergerie, where he meets at the grate of the Palace, Eberle, returning from drinking with Beandiscar. He gave him orders to follow the chair by the street of la Barillerie, himself announcing that he will take that of Jerusalem, in order to get a-head of the chairmen and stop their advance, and that they should meet again at the street of Jerusalem. Roquette does in effect take the street of Jerusalem ; at the bottom of which he overtakes the chair and stops it ; but on only finding Mademoiselle Lavalette in it, he returns with all speed to the Conciergerie.

Scarcely had he quitted the chair, when Benoit, who continued to
follow the chairmen, said, " It is very lucky that this has turned out so."
As for Eberle, instead of executing the order which he had received
from the younger Roquette, of pursuing the chair by the street
Barillerie, he returned to the prison, and went to the chamber of Lavalette under the pretence of assuring himself whether the prisoner had
really escaped. In coming out, he said to his comrades with an affection of zeal truly laughable, " There is still somebody in the cell, and
I'll take care that they shan't come out without proper orders." On
saying, afterwards, that it was very easy to have distinguished Lavalette from his wife, the latter being taller by half a head, and being
asked why he did not make that observation sooner, he replied, " It
did not belong to me to make any observations when the head of the
department was there."

The charge states, that Eberle, being attached to Lavalette's service,
as he had before been to that of Ney, had received from both prisoners
divers sums of money under the head of gratuity. Eberle pretends
that what he received of Lavalette only amounted to 100 francs ; but
on the day of the escape, a search having taken place in his house, there
was found the sum of 1700 francs, which his wife had at first endeavoured to get away from the Commissioner of Police. It cannot be
doubted but that the greater part of that sum came from the bounty
of Lavalette.

[The accusation then proceeds to attach various other circumstantial
proofs of the guilt of these parties. Roquette, the father, it appears,
endeavoured to shift off the guilt from himself to Eberle ; and the charge
does not attach to him any other criminality than that of negligence.
Benoit and Guerin deny the facts, which are not clearly established by
the interrogatory. Madame Lavalette, and the widow Dutoit, were
subjected to interrogations ; the latter preserved the most invincible
silence, or showed, by the few answers she gave, that she was afraid
of betraying her master. Madame Lavalette goes further; she justi-
fies all that has been done, imputing to herself the plan, conduct, and
execution of the enterprise ; and the fertility of her genius furnishes
the accused with more resources than innocence itself sometimes finds.
Lavalette is then stated to have sought the means of escape from his
concealment, not among those whom friendship or gratitude bound to
his family, but among the enemies of the King. It adds, that among
a great crowd of strangers stated to be at Paris, the enemies of social
order, and the disturbers of the age, were Mr. Bruce, an English gen-

Heman, already distinguished by his zeal for **Marshal Ney**; Sir Robert Thomas Wilson, a British Officer with the same predilections; and Hutchinson, a person of the same cast. The latter is said to have been engaged with Ellister, another English Officer, in some scheme of the same kind; and that Ellister would have played a similar part in the present one, if he could have obtained leave from his regiment; Wilson, therefore, was charged with the management of the affair, and the act of accusation permits him to give his own relation of the whole enterprise in a letter addressed to one of his confidential friends in England, and of which the following is a translation —Here follows the Letter from Sir Robert Wilson to Earl Grey..]

SIR ROBERT WILSON TO EARL GREY.

(INTERCEPTED LETTER.)

" It was determined (says the letter) that the fugitive should wear the English uniform; that I should conduct him without the barriers in an English cabriolet, wearing the uniform myself; that I should have a relay of horses at La Chapelle, and proceed from thence to Compiegne, where Ellister should repair with my carriage, into which I should afterwards travel with Lavalette to Mons, by the way of Cambray. I had no difficulty in procuring from Sir Charles Stuart, at my request and on my responsibility, passports for General Wallis and Colonel Lesnock, names which we chose because they were not preceded by Christian names. The passports were duly countersigned by the Minister for Foreign Affairs, but when they were presented for signature, one of the Secretaries asked who Colonel Lesnock was? He immediately replied, it is the father of the Admiral. This object accomplished, Ellister took the passports for Colonel Lesnock, procured posthorses for his carriage; and finally, to avoid all suspicion, took an apartment and a coach-house at the Hotel de Helder, in the name of Colonel Lesnoek. Bruce fortunately learned that the brigade, commanded by his cousin, General Brisbane, was at Compiegne, and that his Aid-de-Camp would quit Paris next day, the 7th of the month, for Compiegne, with the horses and baggage belonging to the General who was then in England. We saw the Aid de-Camp at Bruce's, where we met by appointment. We told him that very particular circumstances obliged us to pass through Compiegne with a person who must remain unknown; we wished to stop an hour or two in a remote and retired quarter. He frankly replied, that he would not trust entirely to us, on the subject; that his existence depended on preserving his situation, but that he would not hesitate to accede to our proposition, particularly since he saw we were interested in the affair. I avow that I felt repugnance at implicating such a person in this affair; but the cause was too important to stop at that consideration, and I encouraged the hope that a day would one time arrive in which it might be possible for me to acknowledge this service. Bruce procured Lavalette's measure, and Hutchinson gave it to a tailor, saying it was the measure of a Quarter-Master of his regiment, who wanted a great coat, waistcoat, and pantaloons, but did not need a suit. The tailor observed that it was the measure of a tall man, and that it had not been taken by a tailor. His remark alarmed me so much that I thought it adviseable to send Hutchinson to say to him, that as the Quarter-Master could not wait till Saturday evening, it was necessary that the clothes should be carefully packed up, and that they would be forwarded to him after his departure. Hutchinson and Ellister took besides all necessary precautions with respect to the horses, and reconnoitred the barrier in a promenade on the preceding day. Every precaution for avoiding accidents being adopted, it was finally agreed that Lavalette should be removed to Hutchinson's lodging's on Sunday, Jan. 7, at half-nine in the evening precisely; and that next day at half-past seven in the morning, equally precise, I should be at his door with Bruce's cabriolet, my servant, the servant on my mare, well equipped, as if I were going to make an inspection. That Hutchinson should ride by the cabriolet, keeping up conversation with us, and that in case any embarrassment occurred, Lavalette should mount my horse and I the mare, in order that we might act more freely and gain in expedition. I should certainly have preferred passing the barriers on horseback; but it was thought that the manner of riding on horseback might attract attention, and that passing the barriers in full day, and in an open carriage, would shew too much confidence to give cause for suspicion. The hour being at last arrived, Ellister, Bruce, and myself, repaired to Hutchinson's apartment, under the pretext of a party for punch; at the moment when Lavalette was to present himself, Bruce advanced to the top of the stairs, Lavalette took him by the hand, and we saw before us this interesting personage. He was dressed in a blue uniform and sufficiently disguised to pass without remark in the apartment of an Englishman. The friend who conducted him did not enter the room, but he delivered to Hutchinson a pair of double barrelled pistols for Lavalette. He appeared at first much moved. We did not permit him to give vent to all his sentiments of gratitude, but a few moments after Ellister and I withdrew, and left him to the care of Hutchinson and Bruce.

" Next day at half-past seven, I was at Huthinson's door. In five minutes I had seated Lavalette, and we were on our way to the barrier of Clichy. We met an English Officer, who appeared supprised at seeing a General Officer whom he did not know. But my servant avoided all questions; I passed the barrier at a moderate pace; the gendarmes looked earnestly at us, but the presenting of arms gave Lavalette the opportunity of covering his face in returning the salute. When we got through the barrier, Lavalette pressed his leg against mine and when we were out of the reach of observation, his whole countenance appeared enlivened by this first favour of fortune.

" The road was full of all sorts of people; but whenever we met the diligence, I began to converse with a loud voice in English, and I remarked that my hat, which was mounted with a white plume, and which Lavalette held in his hand, attracted the notice of the passengers, and withdrew their attention from us.

" Lavalette has such marked features, and his person is so well known to all the post-masters, that the greatest care was necessary. At La Chapelle, where we changed horses, we experienced a moment's alarm at the sight of four gen-d'armes who hovered about us. But Hutchinson, on being questioned by them, relieved us from their importunities by replying, that we were going to choose cantonments for a division of the English army. We were obliged to pass close to other gen-d'armes, who had with them bills containing the description of Lavalette: and here I ought to remark, that these bills had been distributed to almost every individual in France. On approaching Compiegne, I observed some grey hairs projecting from under the brown wig worn by Lavalette. Fortunately I had scissars with me, and I performed the part of his friseur on the road.

" On entering Compiegne we found the serjeant mentioned by Captain Fravell, who conducted us through the town to a quarter extremely well chosen, for we were not incommoded by spectators in the streets. None saw us enter except the soldiers and the English servants who attended us. While we waited for Ellister with the carriage, Mr. F. presented us with refreshment. Finally, towards night as had been agreed upon, Ellister arrived with the carriage which had left Paris by the barrier of St. Denis, and was followed to La Chapelle by two gen-d'armes. I caused the lamps to be lighted as well to shew us our road, as to make it appear that we were under no apprehensions; and having taken leave of our friends, we set out, *well armed, and prepared to make resistance, if we experienced any obstacle.* We were much questioned at the stations for the relays, but we experienced no delay till we reached Cambray, where we lost three hours at the gates, owing to the fault of the English guard, who having no orders for calling the gate-keeper, was not to be induced to do so notwithstanding all we could say to him—a negligence which has already been attended with incon-venience to the Government, and which might have been fatal to us.— In passing through Valenciennes we were strictly examined three times over, and our passports sent to the Commandant. We underwent another examination at some distance from that garrison, and this was the last. We did not stop, except at Mons, where we dined, and made arrangements for the future journey of Lavalette. I wrote several let-ters to facilitate the means by which he may reach his destination, and having provided every thing that appeared best for his health and com-fort, I took leave of him, and returned to Paris yesterday evening by the route of Maubeuge, Soissons, and la Porte St. Martin, after an ab-sence of 60 hours."

" Such is the literal translation of Wilson's dispatch, stripped of reflec-tions which would have appeared displaced in this recital.

" This letter, acknowledged by Wilson, *is confirmed in its details* by the documents in the process; and the interrogatories of the accused explain a number of passages in it. It would appear that it was on the 2d or 3d of January that the first proposal of saving Lavalette was made to Bruce; and Bruce states, on this subject, that a person brought him an anonymous letter, in which after extolling the goodness of his heart, the writer said he was induced, by the confidence which he in-spired, to disclose to him a great secret; that Lavalette was still in Paris, adding, that he (Bruce) alone could save him, begging him to explain his intentions on this subject; that he (Bruce) gave no immediate answer, but promised to send one to a place which he mentioned, and which honour did not permit him to name; that prevented him from putting any questions as to the name of the person who wrote to him, or the place of Lavalette's retreat, thinking that, in an affair of this sort, indiscretion could not be too much avoided. General Wilson, he says, was ignorant of all these details; " it was I who told him of them; it was I who prevailed upon him to unite his efforts with mine in favour of Lavalette ; and if there is any one guilty in this business, it is I. My political opinions might have influenced the sentiments which I expressed on the occasion of Marshal Ney's trial. It was my conviction that the capitulation of Paris stood in the way of his trial. As to Lavalette's affair, I affirm that I was influenced solely by the commiseration with which he had inspired me. There was in his escape something romantic, and so to speak, miraculous, which strongly seized my imagination, and excited a powerful interest in my heart for him.

" Hutchinson makes the same avowals, and expresses nearly the same sentiments as Bruce. He protests that he had not the slightest idea of conspiring against the French Government ; and if he co-operated in Lavalette's flight, it was merely from the wish to save an unfortunate man.

" Sir R. Wilson assigns to his conduct a more elevated object—he wished to efface from the government of his country the opprobrium attached to the violation of the capitulation of Paris ; and he protests that it never entered into his views to make any attempts against the French government : but he avows his opposition to the principles which at present direct the government of his country, and to the political system of Europe, which is no crime in an Englishman : and he adds, that the constitution of his country, its independence, and its happiness, are of much higher consideration in his eyes than the safety of the French government, and the repose of Europe established on the ruin of England.

" But if we wish to know the real sentiments of Sir Robert Wilson, we must seek for them in the correspondence which he held with some private persons in England—a correspondence of which the documents proceeding from himself, or from his brother Sir Edward Wilson, were submitted to his inspection, and acknowledged by him. In all his letters Wilson professes principles the most opposite to all social order, and to the tranquillity of Europe. According to him, affairs have taken a wholly counter-revolutionary course, under the sanction of the courts of Austria and Russia. The dethronement of the King is irrevocable. He gives the epithet of legitimate maniac to a courageous friend who had refused to listen to his dangerous inspirations. He thus closes a letter dated the 28th of December :—" You will soon hear of extraordinary events in Germany."

" The third article of this correspondence is a letter from Edward Wilson to R. T. Wilson, which shews the conformity of principles and unity of sentiments which exist between the two brothers. Edward writes to Robert Wilson, that if it is proposed to overturn the existing order of things, the fire must be constantly kept up, and always visible, like a beacon of alarm, in France and in foreign parts; that matters become daily more favourable for the recovery of the sovereignty and independence of the French people; but that it is to be feared that they should cool; and that efforts be neglected, which, well employed, would necessarily lead to a general emancipation.

" Passing to the means which might weaken the attachment of the majority to the cause of the Bourbons, and insisting on the employment of means, Edward Wilson recommends, above all, the insinuation of a persecution, real or imaginary, against the Protestants—an idea, he says, which spreads like wild fire, diffuses itself like a contagion among the people in general, and engenders a spirit of mortal hatred and contempt for the new dynasty. May this new arm be that of the liberty of all nations !

" He closes his letter by a piece of advice which leaves no doubt as to the dispositions of these implacable enemies of our country. " If, however, our friends show too much weakness, it would be better to attempt nothing ; for unless the great mass of the people put themselves in motion, no result will be obtained."

" The fourth document proceeds from R. T. Wilson. We there find the prognostics of this foreigner as to the revolution which is preparing in France. " There will be bloody scenes before the revolution can be consummated, but the point is fixed, and the impulse given. Revolutionary movements are also preparing in Prussia."

" In fine, the 5th document is the letter from which is extracted the relation of Lavalette's escape. Wilson does not there dissemble the motives which led him to protect that man.

" Robert Thomas Wilson, after having in his interrogatories protested against his arrest, against the form of French criminal inquiry, against the seizure of his correspondence, and against what he calls the inquisitorial system of interrogations, has, however, acknowledged that, according to the principles of the law of nations, he was subject to the empire of the French laws for the prosecution and repression of an offence committed in France ; but he closed the interrogatory with these words :—" It would appear to be forgotten that I am an Englishman, or that the rights of Englishmen is not known. I have given my last answer : let me be brought to trial ; when before the tribunals, I shall know how to defend myself as I ought, and to defend my rights."

In consequence of all these facts, Jaques Eberley, turnkey of the Con-

: Jean Baptist Roquette de Kerguidec, keeper of the Conciergerie; Benoit Bonneville, valet-de-chambre of Lavalette; Joseph Guerin alias Marengo, Robert Thomas Wilson, John Hely Hutchinson, and Michael Bruce, are accused—videlicet, Jacques Eberle, of having on the 20th of December last, in connivance with Marie Chamons de Lavalette, condemned to capital punishment, whose keeper he was appointed, favoured the escape of that prisoner; J. B. Roquette de Kerguidec, of having facilitated it by negligence; Benoit Bonneville, and Joseph Guerin, of having facilitated the said escape by procuring to the convict the means of escaping; and Wilson, Hutchinson, and Bruce, of having, in January, 1816, been accomplices in concealing the said Lavalette, knowing, that he was condemned to capital punishment, and of having thus facilitated and consummated his escape—crimes and complicated offences provided against by articles, 59, 61, 240, and 248, of the penal code.

The Chamber of Accusation has dismissed from prosecution the Widow Dutoit, and Lavalette the wife.

To the above we annex the judicial examination of the parties, on which the bills of indictment are founded:—

INTERROGATORIES OF SIR ROBERT WILSON.

[The first four Interrogatories by Pierre Georges Francois Mounier and Pierre Malleval, Commissaries of Police, on the 13th, 14th, and 15th of January consist merely of the refusal of Sir Robert to answer questions until he had been allowed to communicate with the English Ambassador, and the arguments of the Commissaries to prove, that he ought to answer according to the forms of the law of France, to which he was then subject. The only material point in these Interrogatories is a question, whether he knew a writing presented to him, purporting to be a report made by M. Pozzo di Borgho to the Emperor of Russia on the state of France? Sir Robert answered, that it was not his hand-writing, nor did he know whose it was. He believed the author to be M. Pozzo di Borgho. If not, he did not know who had assumed his name. With regard to Linois, he said that he did not know him, but that he took an interest in his fate because he thought that the capitulation concluded with him did not permit his being delivered up by England to France.]

Fifth Interrogatory.

Q. Did you know Lavalette before his trial?—No.

Q. Have you known him since, and did you see him in prison?—I never saw him in prison.

Q. Did you know for sometime before the 8th of this month, that Lavalette was still at Paris?—I cannot recollect the date; but I think I was informed that he was at Paris on the 3d or 4th January; I had only heard it said so.

Q. Did you not then propose to join in a project, the object of which was to facilitate his escape out of the kingdom.—I was spoken to with that view.

Q. Who was the person that spoke to you?—I was born and educated in a country where the social duties are respected as public duties, and thus my memory is not trained to betray friendship and confidence.

Q. On Sunday the 7th inst. did you not go in the evening to the residence of Captain Hutchinson, Rue du Helder, No. 3, and did you not find yourself there with Lavalette?—I do not, as I before said, recollect dates. 2dly, I regret, on the ground of my preceding answer, the question regarding Captain Hutchinson. 3dly, I have never been in the society of any one where I have heard the name of Lavalette.

Q. In that society have you seen an individual whose name might not have been pronounced before you, but whose figure was unknown to you, and whom, from the air of mystery maintained by Captain Hutchinson, you might have reason to suspect had come there to conceal himself?—I have not said that I passed the evening with Mr. Hutchinson, and I apply again here the preceding reflections.

Q. On Monday the 8th instant, did you not go in the morning to the residence of the Captain; did you not descend for the purpose of mounting into a chaise, which was in the street, near or in front of the great gate, and had you not by your side a man, whom you found in the Captain's apartment?—As from the nature of these interrogatories other persons besides myself may be implicated, I ought to hold myself on the defensive, and keep silence.

C

Q. Do you agree then that you aided Lavalette to quit Paris, and then to go out of France, having him by your side in the dress of an English officer?—I repeat that no person ever appeared before me under the name of Lavalette. It is very true that at the epoch of which you speak, or near it, I accompanied out of France an individual dressed in an uniform great coat, but that is not exclusively confined to the military, and every individual has the right of wearing one. I did not observe that under this coat he had on an uniform dress.

Q. Under what name was this individual known to you? —As that individual had, probably, reasons for concealing his name, I do not think myself authorised to state it.

Q. If you did not know it, what powerful motive could have determined you to take so long and expensive a journey, to accompany him to the frontiers? My motives are not acts of which I feel myself bound to render an account; but I should be ashamed of myself, if friendship, or merely the desire of rendering a slight service to any one who stood in need of it, were not sufficient to induce me to undertake a journey much longer and more fatiguing.

Q. When you passed through Valenciennes, and you wished to obtain a post permit, did you declare your real name?—It is true that I passed through Valenciennes, and I think I mentioned my real name; but in every case, and when I wished to be disguised, the safety of the person accompanying me would sufficiently justify this precaution, if I thought it necessary. On my return to France I never concealed my name, and with my name I passed the frontiers and the strong places.

Q. Do you recognise the permit now presented to you, as that delivered to you at Valenciennes, for yourself and the person who accompanied you?—I do not recollect it.

Q. When you arrived at Compiegne, where you rested, were you and your companion received by an Englishman or a Frenchman?—I cannot, nor will I state what is not purely personal. I owe it however to truth to declare upon my honour, that no Frenchman of whatever rank, at least to my knowledge, was concerned in this affair at the moment when I took charge of the individual; this declaration applies equally to Paris as to the other parts of the journey.

Q. Did you act of yourself, or by the inducement of a stranger, in taking the journey?—I was informed that the journey was necessary to the interests of an individual. I never needed either the efforts or the persuasion of any person to induce me to do an act which I think honourable, and which my conscience approved—honourable, because this act was perfectly disinterested—approved by my conscience, as I am persuaded that every man of integrity, every one of my countrymen, from the highest to the lowest, will approve of it in his heart.

Sixth Interrogatory on the 9th February.

A packet of papers was produced by the Commissaries, and opened, consisting of, 1st, 12 papers, addressed to Lady Wilson—2d, 18 papers, comprising a memoir addressed to Lord Castlereagh, by General Wilson, for the purpose of recalling the public services rendered by the latter in the late war between France and Russia, and documents in support of the memoir—3d, four original letters, also relating to the above memoir—4th, papers, consisting of notes and observations made in a journey of the General in Asia Minor to Mount Ida—5th and last, 64 papers, consisting of different receipts and accounts of expences in English and French.

Also, 1st, a letter addressed to Miss Rhodes, written in English, whom the General stated to be with his wife—2d and last, a letter signed Bruce, without address or date.

General Wilson having read this letter, observed, that it was not addressed to him, and that it was easy to see, from the very respectful expressions in the letter, which were not conformable to the intimacy subsisting for so many years between Mr. Bruce and himself, that it could only have got by mistake amongst his papers.

Seventh Interrogatory of the 14th February.

Q. Was it through a sentiment of pure generosity, as you have stated, that you took part in the escape of Lavalette; or was it not rather with views entirely political, and in consequence of a decided opposition to the acts of Government? A. I begin by renewing my former protest against this inquisitorial system. Passing to your question,

I answer, that I have not named M. Lavalette as the individual whom I accompanied to the frontiers; but at all events, when it was proposed to me to save M. Lavalette, politics had not for a moment any influence on my determination, and my conduct was directed by an imperative sentiment of humanity, which would have induced me to save an enemy under similar circumstances.

Q. You will agree, however, that the indifference which you must have for a man who was unknown to you, and the deep aversion which you do not conceal for the Government, it might naturally be believed that this latter sentiment might alone regulate your conduct in this affair? A. I have answered as to facts, I am not to occupy myself with a possibility with regard to the profound aversion which I am so gratuitously supposed to have for the French Government. I declare that I have never interfered with any act of that Government, in which the honour and good faith of my nation were not interested, and that I had a right, as an Englishman, to criticise such acts.

Q. Why then in the affair of Lavalette, an affair foreign to your Government, did you employ yourself in casting odium upon persons whose duty proscribed to them the prosecution against him; why did you treat them as persecutors who multiplied their efforts to ensure their sanguinary triumph; why did you add that they had discovered the trace of their prey, and that the escape of Lavalette had served to render these monsters more furious? A. Respecting the first article of this interrogatory, I answer that the affair of M. Lavalette, abstracting the part I may have taken in his escape, was not foreign to an Englishman; there existed a Convention signed by an English General, and ratified by the English Government, and to try M. Lavalette, was a manifest violation of that Convention. I am not aware that I used the words which you have stated, but of them you must furnish proof. As to any thing further, I wish to avoid all political discussion, but as you take the initiative, I do not refuse to answer.

Q. The proof which you require results from the letter now presented to you, do you acknowledge it? A. Denouncing this greater crime by which the French Government had seized a sealed letter addressed to a Peer of the Parliament of England, I acknowledge it. I declare that my object is accomplished. The silence which I have maintained, and with which I have been so much reproached, had no other motive than to put the French Government to the necessity of itself unmasking its shame and its guilt by producing the intercepted letter, and which long since I knew to be intercepted.

Q. It would appear as if the honour of your country were not the only consideration to which you would have yielded in this circumstance, since you put yourself forward and justify it by the catastrophe of Lavalette, which you regarded as dishonourable to the cause of liberty and humanity? A. These two words, liberty and humanity, afford the proof of my explanation. In fact, the word liberty, well understood, expresses respect for the laws and for justice; these laws were outraged by the violation of the Treaty; and it is therefore with reason that I regarded the cause as that of liberty united to humanity. The subsequent phrases will still further support the justness of this interpretation, since I express the wish that England will escape the shame of again participating in an assassination, and that every honourable and independent man in Europe may have at least once the opportunity of rejoicing in these times of mourning and ignominy. There was no occasion for me to detail the different sentiments which animated me, and according to the order in which they presented themselves to my mind, I merely wished to give a general representation, and there is a great distinction to be made between the brevity which essentially belongs to a confidential letter addressed to an enlightened friend, and the developements which a letter ought to contain that is intended to be submitted to public consideration.

Q. Ought not the expressions which you employ to designate the persons who acted by the orders of Government, and the hatred that is to be perceived in the manner in which you speak of the Government itself, to induce a belief that the escape of Lavalette was not with you a principal object, but simply a means, a commencement of the execution of an otherwise vast project of a conspiracy antecedently formed and determined upon, for the purpose of destroying or changing the Government, or the order of succession to the Throne? A. The expressions which I used, originated in the spirit of vengeance which I remarked in the persecutions directed against Marshal Ney and M. Lavalette, persecutions which have always, appeared to me an outrage on the honour and good faith of the English nation, identified with the Convention of Paris. I never intended to point out individually either the agents of Government, or any other person, as blameable for the persecutions at which I revolted, but I meant to speak generally of all those who with a furious or at least exaggerated zeal, persisted in demanding blood, and opposed themselves to the wish which had emanated from the heart of the King in the face of the whole world, to exercise clemency towards M. de Lavalette.

Q. How can you escape from the strong presumption which is raised against you, of having wished to destroy or change the Government, you having yourself furnished this reasoning, and having, in the letter which has been produced, not dissembled that the facts which you relate may cause you to be suspected of clandestinely conspiring ; a suspicion which you announce your intention of preventing, by communicating to the Duke what you have done ? A. My avowed and acknowledged political opinions have always been, to let every independent nation alone, and not to meddle with the affairs of Government ; but I have seen with pain the English Government sacrifice the English Constitution, in order to connect itself with French policy. I should have rejoiced in the cessation of this connection. I have never entered into any conspiracy or association against the French Government, I have limited myself to the confiding to the breast of friendship the thoughts and desires with which circumstances inspired me ; it is the birthright of an Englishman, and no one can deny it him when he merely exercises it without accompanying it by any act prejudicial to Government. The Duke, respecting whom there is a question in the passage which had been quoted, is the Duke of York, brother of the Prince Regent, and Commander in Chief of the English Army. The desire which I indicate of communicating to him what I had done, in order to do away all suspicion of clandestine conspiracy, is the best proof I can adduce of the purity of my intentions.

Q. Does not one of your friends, in an answer addressed to you, consider it as beyond a doubt that the nation was strongly indisposed against the Bourbons, and does he not seem alarmed at the want of a demonstration of discontent in this respect?—A. This question has been discussed in England since the re-establishment of the Bourbons, and is still discussed there, but I must see the letter of which you speak to enable me to enter into further details.

Q. The exhibition of the letter cannot be of any importance to you, my object at this moment in recalling to your recollection the answer is, to induce you to perceive the presumed, or rather the well known, sense of the letter which provoked it, and of drawing this consequence, palpable to the eyes of the most ignorant persons, that your opinions were in unison with those of your correspondent, a'though they were in contradiction to those of your own Government, those of France, and I may add, those of all who are the friends of tranquillity, and the happiness of nations? A. 1st, I protest against all responsibility for the correspondence of men free born like myself. 2dly, I oppose the logic of the induction. In fact, if the person who wrote to me had been convinced of the conformity of our opinions, he would not have taken so much pains to develope his own, and to induce me to participate in them. Lastly, not to agree with the policy of his Government is no crime in an Englishman; and I frankly confess, that the constitution of my country, her independence, and her happiness, are superior to every consideration for the safety of the French Government, and the tranquillity established on the ruin of England.

Q. What you call liberty of opinion rests upon a principle to which our Government and our Constitution render equal homage. The law interrupts no person on account of his private opinions, unless they are delivered with the intention of disturbing the public tranquillity. Such is the character which may be remarked in the strange words which I find in this letter, and which I am about to recall to your recollection,—" If it is proposed to overthrow the present order of things the fire ought to be constantly kept up, and always visible, to serve as a beacon of alarm in France and foreign countries." A. I demand a sight of this letter before I make any reply, both for the purpose of ascertaining the writer, and judging of the motives which might have induced him to make use of such expressions.

Q. There it is; do you recognise it? A. Yes. The writer has authorised me to name him: he is my brother. The passage you have cited is a piece of reasoning purely speculative and hypothetical, without any present object; and his intention, which is proved by the rest of the letter, was only to establish the accuracy of his calculations on the state of France and England.

Q. The passage which precedes appears to me to repel this interpretation; and there appears much less of hypothesis than of actual fear in the expression. "There reigns in the provinces a degree of tranquillity that may degenerate into a positive adherence to the views of the Sovereign?" A. It is not "the views of the Sovereign," but "of the Sovereigns," which gives an entirely different sense. I am not obliged to defend my brother; he is able and ready to defend his own cause; but my brother, being an enemy of the system on which the Allied Powers have acted, which he thought calculated to produce much evil and no good to his country, has expressed his fears lest the present system should become confirmed; and, to arrive at the end he proposed, he wished to see all the people of Europe interesting themselves in their own affairs, and regaining what he calls their Sovereignty, which is the basis of the British Constitution. This letter, written in English, and never publicly circulated, cannot be cited as an unlawful act against the French Government.

Q. This correspondence appears to me to have established between your brother and you a sort of consolidation and identity, which makes you mutually responsible for your opinions; it proves that there not only existed in both of you an opinion hostile to the Government, but a plot and a real intention to effect its overthrow; of this I find an unanswerable proof in the last paragraph of this letter, where your brother, seeing but too clearly that actions were wanting to support his opinions, says, "that he must have actions to establish his hopes; but if our friends discover too much weakness" (and this shows that they were on the point of action), "or unless the great mass of the people besties itself first, every thing that follows will be of no effect."

A. First, I repeat always my first protest against any responsibility for opinions which did not proceed from me;

secondly, I believe, for the following reasons, that my brother does not speak of France in this paragraph. He is recalling to my recollection a critique which I had made on Perry, the Editor of the Morning Chronicle, and he has not any acquaintance in France which could justify the expression, " our friends." Besides, it would be absurd to suppose that a man who lives in England, in the country, at a distance from all business, could or would enter into a plot in France. He always recurs to the desire, which was perfectly allowable in him, of seeing the political system of Europe changed. If his letter had any political object, we should not see his family affairs, and other indifferent matters, mixed up in it ; and, what proves that there was no conspiracy between us, is his adding, " I am tired of your sentiments and your violent opinions ;" from which it is easy to conclude, that nothing was passing between us but a communication of opinions. Besides which, if the whole letter be read, it will prove much better than each separate passage, that it relates principally to the situation of England, and to the re-establishment of its independence, distinct from its present connexions with France.

Q. Did not one of your friends, in a letter which he wrote to you last November, testify his regret " at not seeing some prominent chief appear in France in a situation to please; and that submission to which the French people showed itself so disposed ? A. It is possible ; the English journals give an incontestible proof that this desire exists in one party, and I have friends of all parties ; but I do not remember having received such a letter.

Q. Did not you say in the presence of many persons on frequent occasions, and did not you write to your brother Sir Edward Wilson, that the dethronement of the Bourbons was inevitable ? A. It is possible : but always on conditions understood and antecedently expressed, in case of a system of severity being persisted in, framed only to estrange the hearts of the French from their King.

Q. Did you not in another letter announce the news, at once doubtful and alarming, that gloom increased every day in Paris, and that every thing bespoke the approach of a crisis ? A. I never correspond with any but my fellow countrymen, and it is possible I may have transmitted to them the impression which I thought I had remarked in Paris, and which did not escape the English journalists, and which at last was announced even in the House of Commons.

Q. Does not this language refer rather to a conspiracy antecedently averted; and does not this interference result from the following expressions, which cannot belong to a vague and indeterminate proposition. "The blow which will be struck will be heard in a terrible manner, and I hope that the people of Europe will not be deaf to the appeal that will be made to them." A. I have always denied the existence of any plot within my knowledge. I protest against these extracts without date, and mangled from the body of the letter; I repeat, that, as an Englishman, I had a right to communicate my political opinions to my fellow countrymen, and that I am an enemy to the system now established in Europe, so detrimental to the interests, the honour, and the constitution of my country; I declare that I do not recollect the passages cited; but these very passages only announce what I think will still happen in France; the appeal is not to the French people, but to all the people of Europe, in support of the principles I have just announced.

Q. Why, if you have no desire to interfere in the affairs of France, do you announce so ardent a wish to introduce there, and to cause to be translated into French, the political articles of the Edinburgh Review? A. I don't know that I ever expressed this wish; but the work being written by the most enlightened men in England, and containing an abstract of all the books that are published, there, I may have desired to see its circulation in France, at the request of many of my friends.

Q. Without renouncing the inferences which may be drawn against you from this correspondence, did not you yourself, in the month of January last, write with an enthusiasm, and in language which was formerly among us—that of the most ardent friends of revolutions—" The general cry is always, ' they will be turned out ;' this cry has resounded even in Dowing-street, *ore rotundo ?*" A. It is possible I may have done so, but I do not recollect it; if it is true that I made use of such expressions, they must have alluded to some new Envoys either to or from the British Government. What makes me clear on this point is the expression Dowing-

street, which means the seat of Government ; and the words
" they will be turned out" had probably an application al-
together foreign to the French Government. I must add,
that I have not formed my language nor my opinions in your
revolutionary schools ; both are conformable to the true principles of English patriots.

Q. These articles contained political principles, which, according to your own admission, could not be circulated except by manuscript copies, which for this reason could not
produce so much good as might have been hoped from their
publication. By these words " so much good," did you
not mean the agitation of men's minds, and the circulation
of ideas dangerous and subversive of government ? A. First,
England would not permit the publication of a work which
contained dangerous principles ; secondly, The Edinburgh
Review is not confined to politics, and, besides, appears only
quarterly ; thirdly, as an Englishman, I have been brought
up in the opinion that political discussions produce no evil,
and are the soul of tempered liberty and public good.

Q. Can you explain the nature of the extraordinary events
which you announced we should soon hear spoken of in Germany ? A. The judicial curiosity of France ought to confine itself within the limits of its own territories ; besides, I
cannot answer without seeing the pieces from which these
expressions are taken : so far from dreading, I ever solicit
publicity, provided it be of the whole that I may have said
or written.

The accused maintains that his answers contain the
truth : he persists in them, and on their being read, has
signed them with us and the clerk, and has also signed
and inscribed with a *ne varietur* the two letters which we
have shown to him.

Eight Interrogatory.—Feb. 20.

Q. Do you recognise, as having written them, the three
letters which I now show to you, one dated the 6th of last
December, the other the 28th of the same month, and the
third the 6th of last January : and do you consent to sign or
inscribe them with a *ne varietur*? A. Renewing my first
protest against this interrogation, and my complaints against
the crimes committed by the Government for the purpose of

corrupting my domestic, and violating the sacred secrecy of letters shown to me, as being written at the time when the city of Paris was occupied by the Allied Armies, and principally by the English troops, and containing the news and reports circulated in diplomatic and military societies, and obtained in any secret or unwarrantable manner, and only written with the intention of giving my brother and Lord Grey interesting accounts, which they would sooner or latter have received by the Newspapers, I consent to sign and inscribe them with a *ne varietur*.

Q. It is no business of mine to examine here the merits of the complaints that you think you have a right to make on the violation of the secrecy of correspondence, or to explain the means by which your letters may have fallen into the hands of Government; but I ask you, if a person has any right to complain of the neglect of ordinary rules, when he may himself be suspected of having broken through them; if the Government is bound to respect the correspondence of a man, when there is reason to believe he regards, not the repose of Government; and of having violated the laws of hospitality. I would ask you, if, in such in exigency it has not the same right as every private individual, the natural right of defence; if it is, in fact, more to be blamed than one who, when his life is attacked, employs in defence the same weapons as his aggressor, although such are prohibited in ordinary cases? A. The Government ought at once to be the protector of law and the support of morals; but it cannot commit a greater outrage on them than in suborning a domestic, and engaging him by base reward to violate his duty towards his master. But, in truth, the fruit of this crime has been nothing more than the discovery of some private letters, written, perhaps, with some indiscretion, inasmuch as the news which they transmitted was not well ascertained; but which ought not to give umbrage to Government, as they did not expose it to any danger, considering that there was no mention of any thing that was not the subject of public conversation, and probably repeated in all the lettters addressed to England.

Q. But did not you add to these public reports your own private sentiments? Did you not even suffer to appear a want of respect for the person of the King, in saying, for example, " Lord Wellington, seeing he could no longer support the idol he had raised," &c.? Do you not admit that this last expression could only have been employed in a degrading sense;

and in a sort of irony injurious to his Majesty? A. First, the King of France is not my King; secondly, I may make use of the same expressions in speaking of the King of England, without any offence or crime, supposing an ironical idea were attached to them; thirdly, I will not enter into any discussion on private letters intercepted in the manner I have reprobated. I wrote what I thought, not what I did. I cannot be prosecuted for my credulity; but I may reproach myself with having written anecdotes compromising other persons on mere reports, without having ascertained their truth; and I further repeat, that these letters were addressed to my Brother and Lord Grey, whom I considered as my intimate friend, and the most discreet of men. To prove that I was not here for the purpose of exerting myself against the Government, it will be sufficient to read one of the paragraphs of my letter of the 28th December last, conceived in these terms:—
" I seldom go out to appear in any public society, and it is full six weeks since I have been any where but in the society of my best friends." And these three letters, taken together, cannot but prove the truth of my preceding answers, that is to say, that I was indignant at the infraction of the convention; that I wished publicity to the discussions of Parliament, in order to instruct the people on the Continent; and that I thought a throne planted on foreign bayonets, stood in great danger of falling, inasmuch as it did not take its natural basis in a system of clemency and respect for good faith. As an Englishman I had a right to express myself thus, particularly under actual circumstances, when the re-establishment of the King was our own work.

Q. How can it be believed that these expressions were suggested to you by a simple idea of foresight, when, in your letter of the 28th of last December, you " blame your Government for its fear of compromising the cause of the Bourbons and that of legitimacy in general;" and that, in another passage a little below, you speak " of one of your friends who had exhausted your patience, because," say you, " he is become a legitimacy-maniac? A. First, I will not answer a French functionary on the subject of my observations on the English Government. Secondly, I had a right to call an Englishman who adopted the doctrine of legitimacy, either a fool, a maniac, or a traitor, because he outrages the very principles under which the House of Brunswick reigns in England. Thirdly, I am delighted at having this opportunity of repairing publicly, as I have already done in private, the wrong thus offered to his friend.

Q. Your answer does not embrace the whole question I put to you, and which has for its object, not only your observations on the cause of legitimacy in general, but also those that applied to the cause of the Bourbons in particular A. I have already explained myself on my politics, and on my determination not to enter into any discussion on detached passages, of which the sense, considered separately, and by other persons than those to whom they were addressed, might receive an interpretation, different from my meaning.

Q. But at least there are some passages, the sense of which it is impossible to mistake ; thus, for example, when, in this letter of the 6th of December, you announce changes in the French Government, saying, " affairs take a turn quite counter-revolutionary." Is it possible to doubt that you called in question the legitimate authority of the King, and that you regarded it as being established only on a principal of violence and revolution ? A. I shall not enter into a grammatical discussion, which might lead us too far : but I will frankly say, and I hope for the last time, that I have always considered the King of France as re-established by force ; and that, as an Englishman, I do not respect what is called the legitimacy of Sovereigns, when not sanctioned by the people. The word counter-revolutionary, which I have used, was not applied to this legitimacy, but to the change which, according to my opinion, and on the best of my intelligence, was desirable—an opinion in which almost the whole of England to this moment concurs.

Q. Setting aside whatever relates to abstract notions of government, and confining myself to what is personal to the King, I ask why you have attacked his character, so well known to France, and to all Europe, in observing, " I suspect he is not sincere ; that he trifles with his professions of clemency, and that he will support the terrorists ?"

A. Perhaps I have done wrong to the intentions of the King, whom I once personally knew, and who inspired me with a feeling of respect, which has been testified by me in those public services with which he is well acquainted ; but when I saw that the King did not confer the pardon in some degree promised to Madame de Lavalette, and that the King's

Ministers were obliged to abandon their measures of clemency already announced to the Chambers, I at first ascribed this difference between promise and reality to a want of sincerity on his part, especially as he has the right, from his Sovereign character to say " I will." On my arrival in France I brought opinions entirely favourable to his happiness, although I differed as to the means of accomplishing it, and have always thought that amnesty alone could lead to that desirable result.

Q. But after you had conceived a desire to see the Government overturned, you supported your conjectures in this respect with the opinions of Foreign Ministers; and you so litttle concealed the desire, that, in reporting their conversations on this subject, you say in one of these letters, " It is not that I regard them as oracles, but the publicity of their predictions renders them important." It would seem from this that you attached a great value to this importance? A. No desire on my part, similar to that which is supposed, can be inferred from the use of the word " importance," which signifies nothing in our language, or in the passage where I have employed it, more than the authority communicated to the intelligence by the sources from which it proceeded.

Q. But at the end of this first reflection, why do you speak of an individual departed for Milan, in the character of an Austrian courier, to carry the intelligence that the crisis had arrived at maturity; ought it not to be concluded that at this period you were in the confidence of a conspiracy which had for its object the subversion of the Government? A. I announced this intelligence which I had received in the diplomatic circles without any peculiar object; and such a communication I had a right to make: but with respect to any conspiracy tending to overthrow the French Government, I repeat, that my political conduct has been always uniform on that subject, neither to interfere personally, or any country, if not charged with her interests, in the internal affairs of France; and defy the world to prove that I have ever swerved from these principles.

Q. What would appear, however, to establish in a formal and positive manner, that you attached the most lively interest to the circumstance of the courier's departure, and to the object of his mission are the expressions which you add lower down,—that the majority of the people pronounce for the young Napoleon, and that his pretensions, supported by the Russians and Austrians, will finally prevail." A. I had had reason, at this time, to attach importance to the departure of the courier; but some time afterwards I was informed that I had been deceived. I had, however, a right to belive and to announce that a crisis was approaching, when I saw the English troops delay their departure from day to day, notwithstanding the Treaty of Peace.

Q. But did you not proceed farther than conjectures, and speak of a particular and positive knowledge, when you observed, " sanguinary scenes will take place before the revolution can be consummated; but the point is fixed, and the impulse given?" A. I did not say " will take place," but " may take place," which changes the sense of the phrase, and converts certainty into possibility. In other respects the preceding news justified my opinion up to the period when I was undeceived; and this news was not confined to the departure of the courier, but referred to all the political events which formed the subject of general conversation. I shall finally add, that my political opinions (and this declaration is made with perfect candour) had no influence on my decision with regard to the measure submitted to me for saving Mons. Lavalette. My only purpose was to save an unhappy man, of whose life or death circumstances had, in some degree, made me the arbiter, and who addressed himself to me, not only in confidence of my personal humanity, but of the national generosity.

The deposition being read, the accused declared that his answers contained the truth, and that he had nothing to alter or to add. It was then signed by us and by the clerk.

Ninth Interrogatory on the 23d February.

Q. Do you acknowledge as your production, or at least as copied by you, the report which I present to you, and which its title attributes to M. Pozzo di Borgo, Minister Plenipotentiary, and said to be addressed by him to the Emperor of Russia. A. The French Government has calumniated me, or permitted me to be calumniated, in the journals published under its directions, by stating that the original draft of this report was found amongst my papers, written by my hand, and that I was its author. I now tender, in order that it may be joined to the present mimute, the letter which I addressed on the subject to M. Pozzo di Borgo on the 23d of January last, and which I caused to be printed in the English journals.

Q. Did you not at least assist in promoting the circulation and publicity of a work which was calculated to produce so pernicious a result to Europe in general, and to France in particular? A. No: a copy of it was merely lent to me, from which I drew another for the English Government; the copy which is shown to me was borrowed by me to be communicated to a subject of the Emperor of Russia, in order to have his opinion as to the authenticity of the work, which I myself believed to be an official document, on the ground of the extract which it contained from a letter of Lord Castlereagh, which could be known only to one who had access to the porte-feuille of the Emperor. As an historical state paper, I had a right to have it in my possession; but I never lent it to one native of France.

Q. Did you not at least seek to accredit it in declaring your sentiments on the principles therein developed, and which, if enforced, must have caused the subversion of the system adopted by all the Powers of Europe, and have carried agitation and disorder into the bosom of France, whose legitimate Sovereign had been just re-established by all the Allied Armies? A. It appears to be forgotten that I am an Englishman, and that the rights of an Englishman are not understood. My former answer is definitive, nor will I be drawn into a metaphysical discussion of politics. Let me be accused and judged; and when I shall be before the Tribunals, I shall know how to defend myself and maintain my rights.

Q. Do you acknowledge to be of your writing the letter which I present to you, and which has been found among the letters of Lavalette? A. No, It is not of my hand.

Having taken the answers of the accused, we have closed the present process verbal, which he asigned after reading it with us and the clerk; and has also signed and marked with a *ne varietur* the letters which we presented to him; the report attributed to M. Pozzo di Borgo, and the letters which were deposited in our hands.

D 2

Protest of Sir Robert Wilson, mentioned in the minute of the 24th January, and annexed to that minute.

JANUARY 24, 1816.

Before replying to any interrogatories, it is my duty to state the motives which have hitherto dissuaded me from so doing, and those which now decide me to a change of conduct. First, I have received an assurance that Mr. Bruce and Captain Hutchinson have already replied, and I am thus released from all restraint with regard to their proceedings.

Secondly, the application of the moral question no longer existing in its former rigour, I have taken occasion to make my situation known to the English Ambassador, and to transfer to his responsibility the defence of those rights and principles of justice upon which I depend, and which I should have known how to defend to every extremity, without opening this communication.

Thirdly, I was informed that, by my perseverance, in which, after the replies of Mess. Bruce and Hutchinson, and my communications to the Ambassador of my country, I stood alone, I was delaying the trial, and prolonging the sufferings of my friends.

Being impatient also to appear before the courts, yet always protesting in the most solemn manner against the infraction of the laws of nations, the civil and military laws of my country, and the most sacred principles and strongest sanctions of justice, in the adoption of an inquisitorial system; and protesting always against the production and use of any evidence obtained, or sought to be obtained, by these illegal means, in order to prepare and establish the act of accusation against me and my friends; I wait to hear and reply to the interrogatories, reserving to myself the right of giving such answers as seem to me to be proper, not upon a principle of vanity, but for the sake of every person accused in future, and in order to give weight to an affair which must become national.

I have supported the pretensions and the rights of the citizens of Great Britain. I rely with confidence on my country for the protection which I claim.

R. WILSON.

INTERROGATORIES OF J. H. HUTCHINSON.

This day, 13th of January 1816, at eight o'clock in the afternoon, in execution of the orders of his Excellency the Secretary of State, Minister of the Police-General, we the undersigned, Monnier and Malleval, Commissaries of Police of the city of Paris, transmitted the order to lead out and bring before us, Mr John Hutchinson, an English officer, arrested this morning, from the verbal process of our colleague Alletz; and we have interrogated him as follows:

Summoned by his name, Christian name, &c.

He replies: My name is John Hutchinson, native of Wexford, in Ireland, age about 28 years, Captain in the first regiment of grenadiers of the guard, the third battalion, residing at Paris, Rue de Helder, No. 3. I am on actual service, my battalion being in barracks in the Rue Pepiniere.

Q. Do you recognise, as belonging to you, the porte-feuille locked, of which you must have the key, as well as the leathern cover of the same porte feuille which I present you; which two articles contained the papers seized at your apartments this morning.

Having opened the porte-feuille and its cover, Mr Hutchinson acknowledged as his the papers which we extracted and then restored, in order that they might be carefully examined.

Q. Who are the persons that you most frequently visit at Paris?—I am particularly acquainted with Lieutenant Bruce, of my regiment; with Major Ellison, and Colonel Reeve.

Q. Within 15 days has your service called you from Paris?—My service has not required me to leave Paris within 15 days and more.

Q. Have you left Paris in less than 15 days? For what motive? How many days were you absent?—I went on Tuesday last to the Horse at Gonesse, where several English officers agreed to meet for a hunting party. I did not find any one there, the time was not favourable; and I returned immediately to Paris.

Q. Name to me some of the officers who formed the project of that party, and who were to have met there?—Colonel Smith of the 95th Regiment; the son of the Duke of Richmond.

Q. Have you slept constantly at Paris for the last eight days ?—Yes.

Q. Every night ?—Before I continue my replies, I desire to know whether I am speaking to Monsieur Decazes, Minister of the General Police ?

Being answered in the negative, Mr Hutchinson declared to us, that he would not reply to any questions which we might afterwards put to him, complaining that he was deprived of his liberty without being informed of the charges or grievances which led to that rigorous measure.

And all our observations to induce him to answer our questions being useless, and this officer persisting in saying, that if there were proofs of crime against him, he ought to be placed in judgment that he might be punished, but that he would not reply to any preliminary interrogatory.

We have closed the present minute, which he has signed with u s, after having read it.

Second Interrogatory.—Jan. 14.

Q. Have you not taken a very great interest in the fate of Marshal Ney? Have not you endeavoured to withdraw him from the execution of his sentence? Have you no knowledge of projects formed for that purpose?—I never knew Marshal Ney or his wife. I feel interested for him like many others, who think with me that he could not be tried or condemned on account of the capitulation of Paris.

Q. Has not General Wilson communicated to you some project to effect the escape of Marshal Ney?—Never.

Q. What means the note which I present to you, addressed to you by General Wilson, under the date of the 13th of December, commencing in these words: "When these exploits are attempted, *success must be insured*," and where inquiry is made as to proceedings with the Ambassador Stuart to save Linois, and others?—I do not consider myself obliged to furnish the explanation of what you ask; address yourself to the person who wrote that letter.

Q. You left Paris on Monday the 8th of this month, before day; you were not alone? What was the object of your journey? Where did you go? Who were the persons that accompanied you?—I told you yesterday, that, on Tuesday last, I left Paris on horseback to go to Gonesse, on a hunting excursion; it is possible that I may have mistaken the day, and that it was Monday.

Q. But you told me yesterday, that you left Paris alone to go to Gonesse? while it is certain that on Monday last, before day, or at break of day, you left Paris on horseback, in the company of other persons?—I shall give no explanation on that point.

Q. Are you very intimate with Mr Michael Bruce and General Wilson?—I have known Mr Bruce and his family for seven or eight years. General Wilson was aide-de-camp to my uncle; I have known him for the same space of time.

Q. What was the object of the meeting which was held at your apartments on Sunday last, about eight o'clock in the evening, where those gentlemen attended?—We drank a bowl of punch.

Q. Was there no other individual at that meeting?—No.

Q. Did not an individual come to you that night, wearing the uniform of an English officer?—No.

Q. That individual, wearing the English uniform, did he not remain with you, and pass the night with you?—No.

Q. By what barrier did you leave Paris to go to the pretended hunting party at Gonesse?—By the barrier of Clichy.

Q. Did you not take the road to Chapelle-en-Cerval, instead of going to Gonesse?—I will not say where I went.

Q. Was not one of the persons, who accompanied you, in the uniform of an English general officer? Did not you meet, in going through the barrier Clichy, several English officers, who appeared surprised to see a general officer of their nation who was unknown to them?—I remember nothing of the kind.

Q. Did not you go as far as Compiegne?—I will not reply to that question.

Q. How often were you absent from Paris?—I do not consider myself obliged to tell you. If there be any charges against me, let the proofs be produced before a tribunal, and I will defend myself.

Q. The charges, which exist against you, are, that, on the 7th inst, about eight o'clock in the afternoon, the condemned Lavalette, dressed as an English officer, was brought to you; that, on the following morning, he left your house, at the break of day, in an open carriage, having General Wilson by his side ; that you were on horseback, by the side of the carriage ; that you all went out by the barrier of Clichy ; that you passed on to Chapelle-en-Cerval, and went to Compiegne, when General Wilson and the condemned Lavalette took another carriage. You are, in consequence, accused of having favoured the escape of the person condemned to death. What have you to say in justification ?—When I am placed in judgment, I shall produce my means of defence.

No farther questions were asked.

The present interrogatory being read to him, he said, that it contained the truth, and subscribed the two sheets.

Third Interrogatory.—Jan. 15.

A number of queries were put this day to Mr. Hutchinson, and in like manner respecting certain other details of the matters in charge, to almost all of which Mr. Hutchinson declined giving any answer. It concluded as follows :—

Q. Can you give the explanation of a note sent by you to General Wilson, dated the 11th of this month, and which contains divers articles paid by you, as well for horses as for a post chaise, and liveries made by a tailor. I present this note to you. Do you know it ?—I do know it. It is my writing, but I will not state the reasons of the expences which are mentioned in it.

Q. Who are the persons that, the 7th of this month, remained in your apartment, and drank punch with you till midnight ?—All farther questions are useless. I am determined not to repeat the declarations which I have already made.

Q. But you have not been asked, and perhaps you can give some explanation on that point, whether you know the place where Lavalette took refuge, before he came to you ?—I will reply in one word to these two questions. With the exception of a master of the French language, of MM. Livry Martel, wine-merchants, and Sauvage, with whom I lodged, I am not acquainted with any person at Paris.

Q. Was it not you who carried to a tailor the measure which was sent to you by Mr Bruce, and which served to make the habits of an English uniform, in which Lavalette was dressed when he left Paris ?—Mr Bruce never gave me a measure.

Q. What is the name of the tailor who works for you at Paris?—I shall not tell it.

After the denials in which the accused persisted, we have judged it useless to continue this interrogatory; and have contented ourselves with asking him, whether he would sign with us the present interrogatory, and the note referred to in it?

The accused replied, that he consented to sign them both, and he has accordingly signed them with us and the register; after having been read.

INTERROGATORIES OF MICHAEL BRUCE.

First Interrogatory—Jan. 13.

This day, being the 13th January 1816, at three o'clock in the afternoon, we, the undersigned, Pierre Georges Francois Monnier, and Pierre Malleval, Commissaries of Police of the city of Paris, in execution of the orders of his Excellency the Secretary of State, Minister of General Police, repaired to the hotel of the Prefecture of Police, where, being in the cabinet of Monsieur the Inspector-General Faudras, we transmitted a verbal order to the jailor of the depot established in the said hotel, to bring before us the Sieur Bruce, an Englishman, arrested this morning, as appears from the minutes of our colleague Beffara, dated this day, in order that we might proceed to his examination.

Question as to his name, surname, &c.?—I am named Michael Bruce, a native of London, aged 26 years, an English gentleman, residing in London.

Q. How long have you been in Paris? For what object? Where is your place of residence?—I have been at Paris about a year: some days after Bonaparte's departure for the army, in June last, I quitted Paris, and went towards Switzerland; but I was not permitted to leave the frontier, and thus was forced to return to Paris; I was then absent about three weeks. I am at Paris for my amusement; my residence is Rue St George's, No. 24.

Q. Who are the persons whom you most visit at Paris? I mix a great deal in society; I visit a great number of persons; but for the last three or four months I have led rather a retired life.

We then presented to him a little box, in which were enclosed the papers that had been seized in the morning; he acknowledged that the seals had not been touched. We proceeded, in his presence, to open the chest, and unfold the papers. We formed them into two packets, one of English papers of a date posterior to 1814, and the other of French papers of the same date; and we returned all the other papers, together with pamphlets and other printed articles, into the box. And we proceeded no farther. The above having been read to Monsieur Bruce, he said that it contained the truth, and it was signed by us. Closed the above day, month, and year, at five o'clock in the afternoon.

Second Interrogatory,—January 14.

Q. Did you not form the plan of procuring the escape of Marshal Ney?—No.

Q. Did you not take very active steps in his favour?—No; only my personal opinion has always been, that he could not be tried without violating the treaty of Paris.

Q. Were you not in correspondence with Marshal Ney? I saw him almost every day. I had known him for some time, that is to say, ever since I have been in Paris.

Q. Are you not connected with General Wilson and with Captain Hutchinson?—I am connected with both.

Q. Last Sunday, at about eight o'clock in the evening, did you not pass part of the evening at Mr Hutchinson's, Rue de Helder, No, 3.?—I was certainly there; but before I go farther, I beg you to inform me positively of the motives of my detention. We are not accustomed in England to give answers before we know what is imputed to us.

Q. You are accused of having favoured the escape of the convict Lavalette, and of having lent your cabriolet to conduct him out of Paris: what have you to answer?—When I shall come to my trial, I will furnish the necessary explanations.

Q. Are you not connected with M. Elliston of the 5th regiment?—I do not know him.

Q. Where did you send your cabriolet last Monday, half an hour before day?—I will answer when I come to my-trial.

Q. Have you not a cousin who is a general, and commands an English brigade in France?—I certainly have a cousin who is a general, and who commands an English brigade in France. He has not been here these two weeks.

Q. On Saturday the 6th of the month, was not the aide-de-camp of this general at your house?—Was there not a conference at your house between General Wilson, the aide-de-camp, and yourself? What was its object?—I know nothing about it, no such meeting having taken place at my house.

Q. You had not your cabriolet on Monday the 8th of this month: when was it returned to you?—I believe that it has not yet been returned: I am not certain, for I have not been in my stable for several days.

Q. To whom have you lent it?—I will tell in Court.

Q. On the 5th or 6th of the month, did you not send to Captain Hutchinson a measure, according to which he caused to be made a military riding coat, waistcoat, and pantaloons? I will explain myself on this subject before the Court.

Q. Last Sunday evening, did you not see the convict Lavalette metamorphosed into an English officer at Mr Hutchinson's?—I will answer to that before the Court.

Q. Do you know whether the convict Lavalette has left Paris or not?—I know that he has left Paris.

Q. On what day? At what hour? With whom, and how? —I cannot answer this question: but I have no difficulty in saying, that I co-operated in the flight of Lavalette from a feeling of humanity.

Q. How did you co-operate in his flight?—I lent my cabriolet for that purpose.

Q. To whom did you lend your cabriolet?—To the person who accompanied Lavalette in his flight.

Q. Who was that person?—I will not point him out.

Q. Where did you take the measure of Lavalette, by which his English clothes were made?—I never took such measure.

Q. Where, and by whom, was it sent to you?—I will not answer that question.

Q. Before Lavalette left Paris, did you not know for some days where he was concealed?—No. I had not seen him since his arrest, when I saw him at Mr Hutchinson's last Sunday evening.

Q. Was he not dressed as an English officer ?—I believe he was.

Q. Did he go alone to M. Hutchinson's, or accompanied, and by whom ?—I don't know.

Q. Who were the persons present at M. Hutchinson's when M. Lavalette was there ?—I will not answer that question.

Q. Was it not then that you promised to lend your cabriolet, in order that M. Lavalette might set off early the next day; and did you not concert all the measures fit to favour his flight?—Before this meeting at M. Hutchinson's, I had promised to lend my cabriolet for M. Lavalette.

And no farther question was asked. The above examination having been read to him, he said it was true, and signed it with us.

Third Interrogatory.—Jan. 15.

Being asked as to his name, surname, age profession, birth-place, and residence, he answered,

I am called Michael Bruce; my age is twenty-six; I am a gentleman; born in London; residing in Paris, Rue St George's, No. 24.

Q. From your first examination, your answers have been distinguished by a particular character of frankness and good faith. You have said, that, independently of some discoveries which you have made, you would make known the whole truth, when you should be in the presence of justice. You now appear before a member of the tribunal. Are you ready to keep your promise ?—I am ready to tell the truth. I expressed a wish to see M. de Cazes, minister of the police, and, if he can listen to me, I will explain myself with all the frankness that ought to be expected from me.

Q. The forms of justice oppose what you ask. M. de Cazes, as chief of the administrative police, is specially charged with the prevention of crimes, but, once committed, the cognizance of them is referred to the judiciary police, and M. de Cazes must himself refuse, if he was acquainted with your desire to see him. That which you consider a favour

would be an illegal thing, of which you would yourself have
a right to complain. I will receive, as well as he, the information which you can give for the assistance of justice. It is
in the interest of truth that I question you, and not in order to
turn your information against yourself.—I demand, in order
to prese.ve a greater. freedom in my declaration, that the
persons here present may retire, and I will disguise nothing.

And immediately we directed the two gens d'armes,
and the different persons who had accompanied the Sieur
Bruce, to go into the next room. The Sieur Bruce then
went on in these terms :—

I was never connected in friendship with M. Lavalette.
I was never at his house, he never came to my house, yet I
knew him a little before his arrest. His personal qualities,
his sweetness in Society, his amiability, inspired for him, in
my mind, a greater interest than is usually felt for persons
whom one is not in the habit of seeing. His trial, his detention, and the sentence pronounced against him, added to
the sentiments with which I was disposed towards him ; but,
since his arrest, I have had with him no connexion, direct or
indirect. I was entirely ignorant of the place of his retreat,
after his escape. I even thought, that he had a long time
left France. I did not know his wife. I never saw her in
my life. The 2d or 3d of the month, a person unknown
brought me an anonymous letter, in which was exalted the
goodness of my character, and it was added, that the confidence which it inspired induced a determination to reveal a
great secret to me, and this secret, it was added, was, that
M. Lavalette was still at Paris : I alone, it was said, was
capable of saving him, and it was requested I would explain
my intentions on the subject. I did not do so immediately, but
I promised an answer at a place which I pointed out, and
which I think myself bound in honour not to make known.—
I add, that my caution prevented me from putting any questions as to the name of the person who sent me the letter,
and as to the place of M. Lavalette's retreat. I thought,
that in an affair of this nature indiscretion could not be too
carefully avoided. General Wilson was ignorant of all these
details. It was myself who acquainted him with them ; it
was myself who engaged him to join his efforts to mine in
favour of M. de Lavalette; and if there be any person cul-

pable in this business, I declare that it is myself alone, since it was my entreaties which determined him, who is falsely considered as the author of this scheme.

Q. Did not political opinions, rather than personal affections, induce you to serve Lavalette? And did you not do so as a consequence of those sentiments which you had manifested since the affair of Marshal Ney?—I allow that my political opinions operated together with humanity on my conduct since the affair of Marshal Ney: I firmly believed that the capitulation of Paris was an obstacle to his being put on his trial. As to Lavalette, I declare upon my honour, that I was moved solely by the commiseration which his case had excited in me; the adventure of his escape appeared to me to have something romantic and even miraculous about it, which forcibly struck my imagination, and excited in me a kind of lively interest for his person.

Q. Was it not you who procured the measure of Lavalette for Sieur Hutchinson to be sent to the tailor?—I do not know to whom I gave it. This circumstance, which appeared indifferent to me, has escaped my memory; but it is true that I procured it.

Q. Do you know the tailor who was employed to make the clothes?—I do not know; I never saw him.

Q. On the 7th of January, in the evening, when you saw Lavalette at Sieur Hutchinson's, did you learn how Lavalette had come there, and the place from which he had come?—I did not ask him; and I declare that I did not even wish to know.

Q. Do you know, at least, whether he came on foot or in a carriage?—I believe he came in a cabriolet; however, I do not affirm so; when I met him at the door he was on foot.

Q. Do you not know, that as soon as he was introduced into the apartment of Captain Hutchinson, one of his friends came to the door, to bring him a pair of pistols?—I heard it said so, but saw no person; no person entered the room.

Q. At what hour did you quit the apartment of Captain Hutchinson?—About midnight.

Q. To go there, was it not necessary to cross the apartment of the Sieur Sauvage, with whom the Captain lodged? —I never heard the name of the Sieur Sauvage; I never perceived either him or any person of the house, at least to my belief; and I never observed any communication from the apartment of Captain Hutchinson with that of any other lodger.

Q. Was it not in your cabriolet that Lavallette escaped? Has this cabriolet been sent back to you?—I have not ascertained whether the cabriolet has been sent back; I can say nothing positive on this subject; I do not deny that I lent it; the documents which have come into your hands perhaps leave no doubt as to the name of the person to whom I lent it; but it is not my business to make it known. I speak the truth on every point that respects myself personally; I do not think it a duty to do so when it may compromise others.

Q. Was it not you who sent to the hairdresser a sample of hair, and three measures, to make a peruque for Lavalette?—No, Sir.

Q. Yet the contrary would appear to result from the note which I now show you, as well as the sample, and which were found in your porte-feuille?—I certainly acknowledge both the sample and the note; but I declare, that neither of them have any connection with M. Lavalette: I affirm that it was a commission which I received about a year ago from a person named Berthold, who was then at Constantinople, and I believe attached to the English embassy. The letter, I believe, will be found in my porte-feuille, which will confirm this declaration.

The above being read over, the prisoner said that his answers contained the truth; that he persisted in them; that he had nothing to change or to add to them; and signed with us and the clerk, as well the present examination as the note therein alluded to.

Fourth Interrogatory—Feb. 11.

Q. Do you acknowledge the box which I show you, sealed with the seal of the Prefecture, to belong to you?—No, Sir.

[And immediately we broke the wrapper of paper, sealed at its two extremities, one across the box, and the other on the cover; and after opening the box, we put the following question:]

Q. Do you acknowledge the porte-feuille and the several papers contained in the box ;—I acknowledge the box ; as to the papers, the examination of them alone can inform whether they all belong to me, and whether some are not strange to me.

Then proceeding to the examination of the papers, and being convinced of the nature of most of them, and by their dates, that they could not have any reference, direct or indirect, with the affair on which we were seeking information, we occupied ourselves in making a selection of all those which were foreign to our purpose, and we returned them to the box to be shut up again, being first sealed with our seal, and after making a summary and sufficient description of them to point out their contents, in case it should be thought proper to examine them afterwards.

The said papers consist, first, of a collection of divers copies, printed, and in sheets, relative to the affair of Marshal Ney, and of divers other political pamphlets : second, of a collection of family letters, observations made during travels, and addressed to the Sieur Bruce, from Constantinople, Aleppo, London, Geneva, &c. all dated 1813, 1814, and 1815 ; these last before the month of July : third, of a roll of useless papers and envelopes of letters.

We also put up in the box a little list of *agenda* in red Morocco, and the porte-feuille, which contained a part of the papers, on the fastening of which was written the name of the Sieur Bruce.

We then proceeded to the separation of the other papers, and we formed them into two packets.

The first is composed of nine letters, or billets, written in English, which we marked and signed with the Sieur Bruce.

The second consists of 54 pieces, written in French, equally marked and signed by ourselves and the Sieur Bruce.

We lastly put under one cover, four sealed letters, addressed to Monsieur the Duke de Galle, to Madame Richt, at Constantinople, to the Sieur Claudier James Richt, and to Madame the Countess of Aldborough, at Brussels. The Sieur Bruce declared, that he had been desired to convey three of these letters, but he did not know how the letter addressed to the Duke de Galle came among his papers.

We also put under the same cover another letter, unsealed, dated the 10th October 1814, written in French, and not signed.

The Sieur Bruce declares, that he believes he recollects that this letter, addressed to the Princess Staremberg, had been sent to him to be carried to the Princess, in a journey which he had proposed to make to Vienna.

To conclude, the last piece put by us under the said envelope, is a memoir of General Lamarque to the King, dated the 3d of August 1815. With respect to this last piece, the Sieur Bruce declares he had never seen it, and that it could not have been among his papers except by mistake.

This being done, we put our seal and that of the Sieur Bruce on each end of the tape, which bound each bundle to the cover just spoken of; then we locked the box, and put on it the seal, with a wrapper of paper, on the ends of which we also put our seal and that of M. Bruce.

These minutes having been read, the Sieur Bruce signed them with us and the clerk.

Fifth Interrogatory.—Feb. 14.

Q. Was it not political opinions, and a decided opposition to the Government, that induced you to co-operate in the escape of Lavalette, rather than a feeling of affection for him?—I repeat to-day, what I said on my first examination, that a sentiment of humanity regulated my conduct in that affair.

Q. Had you not previously manifested your opposition to the Government, on the occasion of Marshal Ney's trial?—With regard to Marshal Ney, I was influenced by a public and political feeling. I viewed his cause as depending upon the convention of Paris; I thought, and still think, that the honour of my country might be stained by the violation of that convention; it was in this view only, and not from opposition to the French Government, that I manifested my opinion in that affair.

Q. Were you cognizant of a plot framed by some of your accomplices, and which had for its object to destroy or change the French Government?—Such a question can only excite my indignation; all who know me, know well that I am incapable of playing the part of a conspirator. I feel another sentiment of indignation at the very idea of an opinion being entertained of me that I could betray friendship, had it been so confiding as to inform me of a plot, even though I had not approved of it.

The above being read, the accused said his answers contained the truth, and adhered to them.

And the next moment having shown him a letter, signed by himself, without date or address, which was found among the papers seized at General Wilson's, we put the following questions to him :—

Q. Do you recognize the letter which I show to you? and at what time did you write it ?—I recognize it to be my own writing. I do not recollect the time when it was written, nor to whom it was addressed ; moreover, I have no interest in disguising the truth as to this point, on the supposition that it might have some relation to the escape of M. Lavalette, since I have acknowledged the share I took in it.

Q. Will you sign and subscribe this letter, *ne varietur ?* Yes, Sir.

This addition to the interrogatory being then read, the accused said his answers contained the truth, and signed them with us and the clerk, as well as the letter there mentioned.

Sixth Interrogatory.—Feb. 23.

Q. Do you acknowledge the letter which I now present to you, and which was found amongst the papers of Lavalette, to have been written or dictated by you ?—I declare that this letter is not mine, and that I know not the author.

The above being read, the accused declared his adherence, and signed it with us and the clerk, as also the letter therein mentioned.

Q. Did not this person, or some other on his part, observe that Lavalette had forgotten his pistols, and return to your door in order to bring them ?—Yes, Sir ; my servant, John Baldwick, informed me that some person desired to speak to me in the antichamber. I went out to prevent his entering ; I saw a Frenchman dressed in a riding coat, which was partly open, so as to let me perceive a double-barrelled pistol in the side pocket. The first idea which presented itself to my mind was, that all was discovered, and I confess that I prepared to make resistance. I demanded the pistol, and advanced my hand to seize it before he should have time to make any movement. He made no opposition, and only said, " You are then among my friends." I replied in the affirmative, but would not permit him to enter my room, and required that he should instantly absent himself. This was the first time I ever saw this Frenchman; and it was for so short a period, that it would be impossible for me to recognise him. The pistol was the next day forgotten, and left with me by M. Lavalette. On my return I gave my servant orders to discharge it, and I had the precaution myself to take out the flint. The pistol is now at my lodgings, and my valet can produce it.

Q. Had Monsieur or Madame Sauvage, whose apartments you occupy, or any of their servants, or the portress of the house, any knowledge of M. de Lavalette's introduction to your lodgings, and of the stay which he made there during the night;—No, Sir; Monsieur and Madame Sauvage had dined out, at least so I presume, for I remarked that the key was not in the door; the servants live generally in the kitchen, which is one storey lower. When M. de Lavalette entered, there was nobody in my antiroom but Baldwick, and a servant whom I dismissed the following Tuesday.—With respect to the portress, I have never spoken to her, nor do I believe that the persons who called on me ever addressed themselves to her.

Q. Who is the person who, on the next day, between seven and eight o'clock in the morning, came to your door in a chaise, into which Lavalette ascended in order to quit Paris?—I have already said, that I am not compelled to speak the truth except in what relates to myself, nor can I honourably satisfy this question.

Q. When you arrived at Compeigne, was it by a Frenchman or an Englishman that you were received and entertained during the time you remained there?—The same reason forbids me to reply upon this point.

Q. When Lavalette came to you on Sunday, at seven in the evening, was he dressed in the uniform of an English officer?—No, Sir; and I seize this occasion to explain the answer which I made to the prefecture of the police, and which I wish should not be considered as a falsehood. I was asked, whether a person dressed in an English uniform did not call on me, and I replied in the negative; this does not form a contradiction of what I state to day; in point of fact, M. de Lavalette had on his French dress, and it was myself alone who wore an English uniform.

Q. Who are the persons who addressed you, or who brought the uniform?—The uniform was lent me by an officer of my regiment, who was not in the secret, and whom I convinced that Mr Bruce and I wished to carry off a lady from Paris. This officer was called Bruce; he is a Lieutenant of the first company of grenadiers of the royal guard of England.

Q. It appears, nevertheless, according to the note that you have signed, and which I now present to you, that this uniform was furnished to you by a tailor. By the first paragraph of this note it appeared to have cost 152 franks?—That article has nothing to do with the uniform. The tailor had no other orders but to make a great coat, a blue waistcoat, and grey pantaloons. I had given him the measure, without informing him of the object; and I took care to remove from him every suspicion on his part, by telling him that these clothes were to be sent to Abbeville to a Quartermaster: and to fix greater probability on this story, I gave orders to wrap the whole in paper, adding, that I would deliver them to the servant of the Quartermaster, who was then in Paris. The tailor lives in the Rue Pinon; he is a German, and has a small shop. I have forgotten his family name, and know only that his Christian name is Frederic.

This evidence being read, the accused approved of its accuracy, and signed it in our presence.

Fifth Interrogatory.—Feb 9.

This process respected the identification of papers, letters, &c. taken at the apartment of Mr H., all of which were acknowledged, and respectively sealed up by the parties.

Sixth Interrogatory.—Feb. 14.

Q. Why has not your servant answered the summons which we gave him, by appearing before us, and bringing us the pistol, which, on your preceding examination, you declared was to be found at your house?—Because, at the same period, all my people had set off for Cambray. I have no interest in concealing this pistol; I myself made a declaration of it; and I repeat the offer of producing it, if thought necessary, and of writing in consequence to Cambray.

Q. Was not the participation which you had in the escape of Lavalette the commencement of the execution of a digested plot to which you were privy, and which had for its chief object to destroy or change the Government?—No; I had no other thought but that of saving an unfortunate man.

Q. Did you not write a letter to Mr Bruce on Friday preceding the arrival of Lavalette at your lodgings, and which was dated from the Helder hotel?—I never resided at that hotel; it was my uncle who lodged there.

Q. Did you not receive, on the 13th of last December, a letter from General Wilson, in which he said to you, If these expedients are tried, success is certain?—What do these expressions allude to?—I recollect perfectly well having received this letter; but I declare on my honour, that it had no reference to M. Lavalette; it related to private affairs, on which I cannot now enter into any explanation.

The above being read over, the accused said his answers contained the truth, to which he adhered, and signed it with us and the clerk.

Seventh Interrogatory.—Feb. 23.

Q. Your name, &c.?—J. H. Hutchison, &c.

Q. Do you recognise the letter which I present to you, and which was found among Lavalette's papers, to have been written with your hand, or dictated by you?—I know nothing of this letter; it is not of my writing; from the first lines, I perceive that the person who wrote it speaks of a conversation which he heard at Lord Castlereagh's, and I declare that I never was at his Lordship's house in Paris.

The above being read, the accused declared that he adhered to his answers, and signed with us and the clerk both these presents, and the letter which we presented to him.

————

We add the following appeal of Lavalette against the decision of the Court, founded upon the objections he had advanced in his defence ; which rested principally upon the charge laid against him, of his having " usurped a post to which he had no right."

COURT OF CASSATION.

The Court met this day (14th December.)

M. Ollivier, the Reporter, addressed the Court.—Marie Chamans de Lavalette defers to your justice the judgment of the Court of Assize of Paris condemning him to a capital punishment. Whatever be our horror at the attempt which plunged France in mourning, we are here placed above such considerations—Guardians of the inviolability of laws and the forms they prescribe, we must contemplate here only the sacred rights of social regulations.

The Court now gave leave to M. Darieux, the Counsel of the condemned, to speak. He began by a panegyric on the moral character of his client—I am not ignorant, he said, that the Court of Cassation does not pronounce upon the man, but upon the work of the Magistrate. It behoves it therefore to ascertain if M. de Lavalette has been legally tried. In the first place, the indictment charges the crime of High Treason. By whom can this crime be tried ? By the Chamber of Peers, which, by the terms of the 33d Article of the Charter, has alone the right to take cognisance of such offences. It will, perhaps, be objected to me, that M. de Lavalette, in not demanding to be sent before the Chamber of Peers, tacitly recognised the competence of the Court of Assize. But of what signification is that ? The crime is national ; the punishment ought to be equally national. The silence of the accused, the error of the Judges, cannot, even in the case, give to the tribunal a competence that does not belong to it, particularly in an offence which relates to public order. Supposing that the Court of Assize had had the right to try M. Lavalette, it is not less certain that its sentence is null under this first point of view.

The Counsel passed to the second objection.—Nothing proves that on the 21st November the Jury were present at the two Sittings of the night and morning. The *Proces Verbal* announces the resumption of the audience, but it does not state the presence of the Jury. This presence being ordered, it is necessary that the proof should be furnished to the accused.

Third objection.—Nothing is more contrary to the law than the position of the questions. There existed a principal fact, the usurpation of the functions of Director General of the Posts. It was upon this fact that the Jury should have first decided, whereas they begin by presenting to them questions relative to the circumstances of this fact.

Fourth Objection.—The contravention of the 370th Article of the Code of Criminal Institution is striking. There exists no minute of the decree which shews that the Court had decided upon the claim of the accused tending to change the position of the questions. The *Proces Verbal* says, that the Court received the claim, but no minute of a decree declares it.

Fifth and Sixth Objections.—It is notorious that M. Torcy de Villedieu assisted at the trial as a supplementary Judge. But where is the proof that he did not, notwithstanding the text of the law, take part in the deliberation? I ask, what proves that the President of the Court of Assize made known all the presumptions favourable to the accused? A sentence which contains such contraventions cannot subsist; and if the insufficiency of the means of the defender could injure the successes of the appeal, the extent of your knowledge, Gentlemen, and the severity of your attention will in that case re-assure the accused.

M. Mourre, Attorney-General, successively attacked and overthrew all these objections. If we could admit that the objections to the competence of the Court of Assize were good, it would still be too late.—It has never been permitted to deny, after trial, a competence which has been recognised in fact in pleading upon the foundation of the accusation before a Tribunal which has proceeded to the trial, heard evidence, and pronounced sentence. But the objection besides is destroyed by the mere reading of the article of the Charter. It attributes to the Chamber of Peers the cognisance of crimes of high treason which shall be defined by law. No law has yet defined them. The crime which produced the condemnation comes within the order of common right—carried first by a royal ordinance before a Council of War, the condemned demanded to be tried by his natural Judges. This he obtained from the justice of the King—the Court of Assize was essentially competent.

The *proces verbal* of the first sitting expressly states that all the jurors were present. The subsequent sittings did not form distinct hearings, but a simple continuation of the first (for the Court of Assize is held not to break up). The observance of the forms mentioned in the *proces verbal* of the first reading extend implicitly to those hearings which are only its sequel, and the state of things is regarded as being always the same, so long as any change which might take place is not legally proved. In the positions of the questions, the ideas of the spirit and text of the law have been followed. The fact of the usurpation of title and functions, and the fact of implication in the attempt consummated on the 20th of March are, in their nature, so dependent one on the other, so essentially connected by their combination and their result, that it is impossible to separate them. The question, as well as the fact, must be complex. The circumstances ought to be brought forward before the crime, because they are not aggravating but elementary circumstances, and constitutive and creative of the offence.—Without them the crime would not have existed, while in all the other cases to which it has been wished to compare this, the crime might have existed independently of the circumstances. Consequently the Jurors had to deliberate on the fact and the circumstance. The intention of the law is fulfilled.

The Attorney-General easily shewed that the *proces verbal* sufficiently proved the deliberation of the Court of Assize on the Petition of the accused relative to the position of the questions. The insertion of that circumstance even in the context of the Judgment, was therefore superfluous.

It was not allowable to presume that the suppleant Judge had participated in any deliberation, and the silence of the *proces verbal* is a sufficient proof of that. When the President proposed to appoint one suppleant Judge and two suppleant Jurors, to replace those whom any unforeseen accident might prevent from attending to the whole of the

F

discussions, the accused consented. But this measure of precaution, proved unnecessary, as no alteration had taken place, either in the composition of the Court or the Jury. If not that, the *procès verbal* would have mentioned it, but it is silent. Things then remain in the state in which they were at the end of the Court.

The sixth and last objection is answered by the same observation.— It is pretended that the President of the Court of Assize omitted in his summing up, to state to the Jury the observations favourable to the accused. It is legally proved that the President did charge the Jury, and his character, knowledge, and long experience, are sufficient pledges that he could not have neglected any part of his duty. The Attorney-General concluded by moving that the appeal of the prisoner should be rejected.

After deliberating one hour, the Court pronounced a decree, the grounds of which were stated with great force and clearness by M. Barris, the President. Contrary to the usual usage, but according to his particular practice, the President did not read the grounds of the decree, but delivered an extemporary statement of them. The decree, in conformity with the motion of the Attorney-General, rejected the appeal of Marie Chamans de Lavalette.

~~~~~~~~~~~~~~~~~

ASSIZE COURT OF THE DEPARTMENT OF THE SEINE
Sitting of April 22.

Robert Thomas Wilson, Michael Bruce, and John Hely Hutchinson, appeared yesterday before the Assize Court, together with Jacques Eberle, turnkey of the House of Justice; and the other prisoners concerned in the escape of Lavalette.

The trial commenced at 11 o'clock. M. Roman de Seze, son of the Peer of the same name, sat as President of the Court. The other Judges were Messrs. Plaisance, Château, Delaville, Decerney, Depaty, and Demeus-Jury.

M. Hua, the Advocate-General, was charged with the functions of public prosecutor. The accused were introduced, and placed on different benches according to the nature of the different charges against them. General Wilson was in grand uniform, and ornamented with brilliant decorations of seven or eight Orders of different States of Europe, one of which was the Grand Cordon of the Russian Order of St. Anne. Captain Hutchinson wore the uniform and decorations of his rank.

There was a brilliant assemblage of auditors, and particularly of English Ladies.

The accused being called upon to give their names, surname, and qualities, gave their descriptions as before mentioned. M. Bruce said with energy, " I am an English citizen."

The President then observed, that although the three Englishmen relied upon the correct knowledge which they appeared to have of the French language, and did not ask for an interpreter, yet the law of France, always a law of protection, willed that the accused should not be deprived of any means of facilitating their justification, even when unclaimed; the Court, therefore, named to that office M. John Robert, who accordingly took the usual oath.

Mr. Bruce, (*speaking the French language*)—GENTLE-MEN OF THE BENCH AND GENTLEMEN OF THE JURY—I have a declaration to make to you in the name of myself and my two countrymen. Although we have submitted ourselves to the French law in consequence of the accusation against us, we have never lost the privilege of invoking the Law of Nations. Reciprocity among nations is the first Article of all Treaties; and as in England, French culprits have the right of demanding a Jury composed half of Englishmen and half of foreigners, it appeared to us that the same right—or, if you will, the same favour—could not be refused to us in France. With this view, we submitted to eminent lawyers of our own nation several questions, the solution of which might justify the right of which we speak. Strengthened by this decision, we should have been justified in demanding the favour of a Jury half French and half English; but, Gentlemen, the justice which has been rendered us by the Chamber of Accusation (in acquitting us of any plot against the tranquillity of Europe, and particularly against the French Government), we have determined to renounce our right. We, therefore, abandon ourselves fully, and without reserve, to the honour and conscience of a Jury composed of Frenchmen; we do not even make the least challenge. If, notwithstanding, we think it necessary to make a special declaration, it is to express that we only renounce the right as far we are personally concerned, and to prevent any precedent being drawn from our case against those of our compatriots who may hereafter be in the same situation. We cannot and will not prejudice their rights. In faith whereof we have signed our present declaration.

M. Dupin (Advocate for the Englishmen)—Will the Court be pleased to enter this declaration on the record?

M. Hua (Advocate-General)—This declaration is calculated to astonish! To claim in France, for an offence committed in France, the privileges of a foreign Legislature, is to set at nought the first principles of social order; the form in which the pretension is urged does not at all change its nature. We oppose the entering this protest on the record.

M. Dupin (the advocate of the Englishmen) maintained that no French law prohibited the composition of a Jury half of Frenchmen and half of Foreigners, It was a question entirely new, which might fairly be discussed, and might or might not be decided against the accused ; they, however, renounce the discussion, but in renouncing it they wish their declaration to be recorded. They will one day return to their country, and they do not wish to expose themselves to the reproach of having sacrificed the right which eminently belongs to an English citizen—that of maintaining, even in chains, the prerogatives of a free man.

M. the Advocate-General.—To say that they submit to be tried by the French law, is to say, that if they did not submit, the trial could not take place. It is this pretension which I repel for the national honour and interest.— It matters little whether in your hearts you submit to the French Legislation ; *you are submitted to it by necessity.*— Crime is a thing peculiarly belonging to local jurisdiction. The offence was committed in France : the prosecution of it belongs exclusively to the French law : English prisoners, therefore, stand on your defence !—(*Anglois accuses—defendite causam.*)

The Court, after a short deliberation, decided against the claim, and ordered the trial to proceed.

Here the Clerk read the Arret of the Act of Accusation, drawn up by the Procureur-General Bellart. The reading lasted more than two hours.

" He does not dissemble the unpleasant consequences of his enterprise : he was not ambitious to be imprisoned, or to lose his commission ; but he was resigned on both points. He had conceived the idea of communicating what he had done to a *great personage*, in order to avoid the reproach of a clandestine conspiracy : he even asks advice on this subject. He appears to have acquired information of great importance, but waits for a sure conveyance to send it to his Correspondent. He had learned, by the confidents of the Duke of Feltre, that Soult was on the first list of the proscribed, and had written to supprise him of it."

The Advocate-General retraced rapidly the facts of the indictment, and fixed the attention of the Jury on the principal points; he applied himself particularly to the distinction in the cases of the different prisoners.

The President here successively interrogated the accused : their answers referred to the details already given in the indictment.

The President then addressed himself to Mr. Bruce :—

Q How long have you been in France ?—A. About 13 months.

Q. You remained here during the stay of Bonaparte ?— A. Yes ; I left Paris two hours after Bonaparte, when he went to take the command of the army. I did not think it right that an English Gentleman should remain in a country which had commenced hostilities against his own.

Q. It appears that you returned to Paris, and were here on the 28th of June.—A. It was because Marshal Suchet, who commanded that part of the frontier which I wished to pass, refused to let me pass, in spite of a letter which I wrote to him, and I was obliged to return to Paris.

Q. You wrote also to Madame the Duchess of St. Leu, whom you called *Imperial Highness,* although your Government had never recognised Bonaparte as Emperor.— A. It is true that I wrote such a letter; I gave her that title , because it was the one she bore.

Q. You were connected with several persons in the intimate confidence of Bonaparte, particularly the Duke of Vicenza ? A. It is true ; but I do not see what relation these questions have to the affair of Lavalette.

Q. It is not for the accused to judge of the merit or the object of the questions addressed to him ; the President has a discretionary power of putting what questions he thinks proper. Was there not found at your house the original of the answer of the Duke of Wellington to Mar-

shal Ney. You took a very lively interest in Marshal Ney?
—A. Yes? a very lively interest; I do not blush to own
it. The most lively interest during his trial.

Q. Was it to you that the first overture was made of the
plan of transporting Lavalette out of France, and of the
plan of concealment?—A. There was no question of concealment, for that was no longer possible.

(The President explained the justiciary sense of the
word *recele*. It was to shelter a man from prosecution, to
withdraw him from the power of the law, by concealing
him either for a short or a long time.)

The accused here recounted the manner in which he
had been mysteriously solicited to co-operate in the flight
of Lavalette from Paris. If possible, said he, I would have
effected his escape by myself alone; for I could not re-
pulse a man who had put his life into my hands. I, however, obtained his consent to confide his secret to one of
my friends. I will not name those friends; they will name
themselves.

Q. It was you who received Lavalette at the house of
Capt. Hutchinson?—A. I received him when he was conducted to the house of that person whom I have not named.

[Hutchinson, who was close to Bruce, bade him name
him.]

President.—This discretion is very useless, for Messrs.
Hutchinson and Wilson have denied nothing, as you know
by the publication of those pieces which have been circulated in a manner so contrary to our practice. You know
that Lavalette passed the night in the house of Capt.
Hutchinson, and that Hutchinson does not deny it.

Bruce.—It was not myself who engaged Hutchinson,
who authorises me to pronounce his name, to receive M.
Lavalette.

Gen. Wilson *(rising)*—It was I.

The President *(to Mr. Bruce)*—There was found at the
house of M. Wilson a memorandum of an expence of 200
francs, occasioned by Lavalette's journey.

M. Wilson.—Mr. Bruce paid this sum, and sent me the
memorandum at my request.

The President then interrogated M. Hutchinson who
agreed to all the facts that concerned him. It was at his

house that Lavalette slept on the night from the 7th to the 8th of January. There is no trace of the retreat of Lavalette between this period and the 20th of December preceding.

Q. *(to Hutchinson)*—You escorted Lavalette?—A. Yes, on horseback.

Q. You wished no doubt to serve your friends?—A. Not so? I was actuated by a sentiment of humanity.

Q. But you did not take a particular interest—an interest of the heart, in this project, because you gave a memorandum of your expences to Gen. Wilson?—A. I did so, being desired to do so; but I nevertheless took great interest in Lavalette.

The President *(to Gen. Wilson)*—Did you know Lavalette before his escape? A. Never.

Q. You began to serve in Egypt?—A. No; I began service in Flanders.

Q. But you have served in Egypt?—Yes, Sir.

Q. You have spread through Europe, by a celebrated work, violent suspicions against the morality of certain agents of Bonaparte in Egypt?—It is true; I said that which I believed to be truth.

The accused here declared that it was himself alone who made all the dispositions, and took all the measures for the escape of Lavalette; he confirmed all the facts related in the act of accusation; he added that Lavalette was dressed in an English uniform, covered with an English great coat, and mounted with a hat of the English form. Bruce here laid hold of the military cap of Hutchinson, and shewed it to the President, saying it was such as that.

Q. *(To Wilson)*—You knew that Lavalette was condemned to death by a jury?—A. Yes, certainly; it was his condemnation that rendered my assistance necessary.

Q. You knew the crime for which he was condemned, for having suppressed the proclamations of the King, for having on the 20th of March put himself in correspondence with the usurper, and for having co-operated in the return of Bonaparte?—A. We are not agreed as to his crime. I believe that Bonaparte undertook this enterprise without any connexion in France.

Q. It is not my business to institute a political contro-

versy. Lavalette was condemned for having violently seized a public authority ; for having corresponded with Bonaparte, and stopped the King's Proclamations ; and for having deceived the inhabitants of France as to the true situation of Paris. A. Much less of politics than of humanity
entered into my conduct. Bruce, in speaking to me about
Lavalette, addressed himself to my heart. I dare flatter
myself that his hope and confidence in me have not been
deceived. Sir Robert declared further, that Mr. Hutchinson did nothing but by his influence, and that, in what he
then did, he was guided by no political feeling whatsoever,
but only by motives of humanity.

Having said this, he sat down.

The Court then proceeded to the examination of witnesses ; the substance of which is contained in the Act of
Accusation, which we have already given.

After the examination of those witnesses, Madame Lavalette was introduced. Her entrance was announced by
a murmur, expressive of the interest and curiosity of the
audience. When she appeared, Wilson, Hutchinson, and
Bruce, saluted her with a profound bow.

The emotion and mental distress of Madame Lavalette
were so great, that, when interrogated, she could scarcely
articulate her own name ; and when asked her age, she replied, " Twenty-seven, I believe."

After having collected her ideas for some moments, she
said " The distress which I feel does not proceed from any
fear, but from a kind of alarm on seeing myself before a
Tribunal, and amidst so large an audience."

The President—Madame, It is not public justice which
has summoned you here ; it is some of the accused who
have invoked your testimony.

Madame Lavalette—I declare that the persons who have
called me, contributed in no respect to the escape of M.
Lavalette ; no one was in my confidence ; I alone did the
whole.

Some details were asked of her as to certain circumstances, which, though minute in appearance, might throw
light on several facts of the accusation. She replied, that
she did not recollect them, and assigned for her defect of
memory, an excuse which will be easily admitted: " At

that moment," she said, " I was too much occupied with the execution of my plan to pay attention to what was passing around me."

M. Claveau, Eberle's counsel, requested her to fix precisely the moment of the disguise; and to state whether it was already executed when Eberle came to receive his last orders.

Madame Lavalette, who was unaware of the consequences of her answer, said, " at that moment the disguise was completed, because M. Lavalette had got off."

The President.—I will put to Madame only one question, Have you ever known or seen these Gentlemen (the English) or any one of them?

They immediately rose, and Madame Lavalette, after having looked at them for a moment, declared that she had never known nor before seen them.

Mademoiselle Lavalette was then introduced; as she was not quite 14, the administering the oath to her was dispensed with. She answered to the first questions in so feeble a voice, and her embarrassment appeared so painful, that the President, after asking the consent of the prisoners, signified that she might withdraw.

The Court rose at half-past five, and was adjourned till to-morrow at nine. M. Claveau is Counsel for Eberle; M. Blaque, for the gaoler, Roquette; M. Mauguin, for Bonneville; and M. Dupin, for the three Englishmen.

Second Day—Tuesday, April 23.

This day the examination of witnesses was continued.

The Colonel of the Staff Grisenoir, and the Major of gen-d'armerie, Jensac attested the one verbally, and the other in writing,—that, having been charged with the command and internal superintendence of the Conciergerie during Marshal Ney's trial, they saw Roquette constantly exercise and recommend the most exact vigilance; and these witnesses were convinced that the attachment of this gaoler to his duties was supported and increased by his excellent principles and opinions.

Similar testimony was given for him by several Inspectors of Police.

The widow Dutoit, aged 72, confidential woman of Madame Lavalette, called for the accused, declared, that she did not recollect any of the circumstances which preceded or accompanied the fact of the escape; she did not even recollect who the person was that introduced her without permission into the chamber of the convict. It was in vain some of the Judges and Jurymen pressed her with questions—in vain the President reminded her of the oath she had taken—she persisted in saying, that a severe indisposition prevented her from retaining any recollection. M. the President, unwilling that she should perjure herself, dismissed her, observing, " Something, I know not what, prevents me from arming the hand of justice against you."

The woman Gorse, a neighbour of Eberle's wife, stated, that at the period of the entrance of the Allied troops into Paris, the wife of the accused shewed her a sum of 1200fr. about which she appeared alarmed, and consulted her as to the means of placing it in safety.

Laporte, one of the ordinary chairmen of Madame Lavalette, and who, on the day of the escape, had been replaced by Brigant, deposed, that the day after, when he asked Brigant why he had not finished his job, the latter made no mention of offers having been made to him, but excused himself by saying, that two days before he had made a severe journey, which had strained him.

Here ended the examination of the witnesses, upon which Mr. Hua, the Advocate-General, rose and addressed the Court in nearly the following terms:—

A criminal, he observed, a convict, has escaped from justice: happy for him if he escape from remorse, and if he can find a place where he may shew with serenity a forehead which the judicial thunder has scathed: a wife has saved her husband; let it be the subject of her joy, provided the act which has done her honour shall not compromise any one. It is easy to account for the share which some of the accused, on whose fate you have to pronounce, took in this enterprise; their sentiments, their duties, their interests, explain the part which they played; but how happens it that these three foreigners are before you ? What was the nature of the interest which they took in saving the convict? They were neither the relatives, the friends, nor even the acquaintances of Lavalette. Will they say that they acted from views of humanity ? But how characterise that humanity which displays itself only by a contempt of public order, and the infraction of the laws ? How appreciate that humane intention, if the correspondence of the accused proves, that hatred of our laws is in their hearts ; that our repose is odious and disagreeable to them, if they saw not in that escape any thing but an outrage on authority, a seditious means of fomenting a revolution ? If this act, feeble in itself, was a sort of initiative of the project, it became the duty of public justice to search it to the bottom, and to trace to you the machination to its very focus. The Advocate General applied himself in the first instance to compare and appreciate the facts relative to the escape of Lavalette, and with great order and precision marked the share which each of the accused had in the act, and the motive which might have actuated him. He distinguished, with the most judicious equity, between crime and simple offence, and assigned to each, as it were, the punishment which he incurred, without, however, depriving any one prisoner of the hope of the indulgence of the Jury. He then naturally came to the offence of concealing the convict, and it was here that the three Englishmen came upon the stage.

The first part of this affair is intelligible enough. All the facts have a resemblance to every day occurrences.— We have a woman who saves her husband—a guard who neglects his charge—another who allows himself to be corrupted—a domestic who devotes himself for his master —and a mercenary who is seduced by the attractions of a great bribe. The origin of all this is to be found, not in the principles, but in the passions and affections of men. Hitherto we have recounted a history—we now come to a romance. You have been seized with this idea ; you have put the first question to yourselves—why were the English engaged in this affair ? Their interference cannot be explained on ordinary principles. They themselves declare and protest on their honour, that, before their participation in the crime, they did not know the indi-

vidual in whose service they exerted all their efforts.—
We are bound to believe their assertions, but it is incum-
bent on them to explain the motives of their conduct.—
One of them (namely Bruce), who was the first confi-
dent in this affair, will declare, that, advised of the retreat of Lavalette in Paris by an anonymous letter,
in which he himself received compliments, he believed,
according to the declarations of the said letter, that he was
the only person who could save him. At first his pride
was flattered; then his natural sensibility was excited; and,
last of all, his understanding was exalted by discovering
in the escape of Lavalette something romantic, and even
miraculous, which powerfully struck his imagination, and
impressed his heart. The other (Hutchinson) did not feel
the same decided warmth of fancy. It was, in his mind,
a sentiment of humanity which exerted itself in the cause
of Lavalette; he only yielded to the desire of saving an
unfortunate man. The third (Sir Robert Thomas Wilson)
derives the motives of his conduct from higher considerations. He imagines that the honour of his own Government would have been destroyed, if a sentence of the Royal
Court of Paris was executed. He does not concern himself with the rights of Sovereignty, or the unquestionable
authority of the judicial power in France over a French
subject. Ah! truly these are common rules. The capitulation of Paris, however, is his law. It has been violated, and he conceives it to be his duty to clear his Government of the opprobrium which that violation casts upon it.
Thus the convict was to be saved for the honour of justice
and that of England. You shall soon see how much truth
there is in all this; but, before we discuss his intentions,
we must establish facts.

The convict had escaped from prison, but it was necessary to escape from Paris. He could not here be concealed from an active Police—a Police which never sleeps—
which has a hundred eyes to see, and a hundred hands to
apprehend—which always succeeds in seizing the object
whom it pursues. It was necessary, therefore, that Lavalette should leave Paris, and even France. You are already acquainted with the plan and the details of his escape. He effected his escape in the uniform of an English officer, and accompanied by English officers as far as
C———, one of whom conducted him as far as Mons.

Thus Bruce, who received the first confidence, goes to communicate it to Hutchinson, then to Wilson. The plan was arranged between them, and each of them engages to act his part in co-operating for its accomplishment. Bruce is to procure the measure of Lavalette: Hutchinson orders the clothes; Wilson is to secure two passports under feigned names. One of them engages post horses, another lends his carriage, and the third his lodgings to receive the convict on the night previous to his departure; and they all assemble on Sunday the 7th of January for the final accomplishment of their object. The pretext of their meeting was an arrangement for a hunting party; but, at nine o'clock at night, an unknown individual announces Lavalette, who is introduced, passes the night in the lodging, and sets out with them on the following morning. I shall not trouble you with an account of the journey. I shall not descant on the measures they took before setting out, or the boldness and grandeur of enterprise which they disclosed. I shall lay before you the precautions they took against accidents—the led horses for the purposes of flight, the arms for the purposes of defence; in a word, all those circumstances which invest an expedition with adventure and honour. I will lead your attention to one point: I mean the asylum given to the culprit before his departure from Paris; and that given upon the road, in a house at Compiegne. This is called, in the language of the laws, a *recele*. The simple fact of concealing a condemned criminal is in itself a crime. The English laws are not more liberal than ours. They do not understand by humanity that generosity which counteracts the rules of public order. Blackstone, after having marked the distinctions which it is necessary to make between the crimes of accessories and principals, distinguishes farther those who are accessories before and after the commission of the crime. He says, in chap. iii. p. 29, of his Treatise, " The accessory before the crime is he who arranges, counsels, or commands it. After the criminal act is committed, a person may render himself accessory to it by giving an asylum or protection to the criminal, or by procuring his escape in any possible manner." This is the law on the subject of yielding protection to a convict escaped from justice, which we call a *recele*. I have cited the authority of this author, it is only in the character of written reason; for it is sufficiently understood that there are no other laws in exercise regarding crimes committed in France but French laws. Who, then, can here dispute their empire? I shall not, certainly, undertake to prove our right of jurisdiction over these foreigners. The opposition of the accused Wilson, his protests against our procedure, his perpetual invocation as an Englishman of the judicial forms of his own nation, are all connected with pretensions which cannot be listened to in matters of criminal justice. Criminality gives the right of punishment; it bestows jurisdiction, for it aims at public order; and there is not a nation on the earth, there is not a social body, which does not in the highest degree possess the right, and lie under the obligation to punish those who infringe it. Every man should know, that in planting his foot upon a foreign soil, his first duty is to observe its laws. Does he not enjoy their protection—do they not watch over his safety—and can he invoke their aid in one case, and brave their authority in another? Good sense alone renounces such an error. As to the forms of inquiry, as to the mode in which the Criminal Tribunal is regulated which applies the laws, it is clear that they depend upon the right of sovereign jurisdiction. Every State has its justice, and also its mode of administering it.

It is said, that a Frenchman accused of having committed a crime in England is entitled to have one-half of his jurymen French. This is a privilege, doubtless. Here, however, you will have no need of this privilege; it will be useless to you : justice does not inquire whether you are natives or foreigners, it views you only as accused, and it will know no other distinctions but those which proofs shall establish between innocence and guilt.

I proceed to the examination of these proofs, but I must first touch upon the head of accusation.

Bruce, Hutchinson, and Wilson, are charged with being accomplices in concealing Lavalette, knowing that he was condemned to die. The consequence is, that they facilitated and consummated his escape. And here I must anticipate a dispute about words. It will be said, that the escape was the act of issuing from prison; that outside the gates it was consummated; and that thus it is false to charge the accused with having facilitated and consummated a thing already done.

But we must look to the sense in which they are inculpated. It must be true, that the escape was facilitated in this sense—that the recapture of the convict was rendered impossible. In vain did the police make its searches at Paris, when the convict was no longer there; in vain, also, did it search for him in France, when he had passed the frontier; and thus the escape was consummated.

But the fact which constitutes the crime which stands at the head of the accusation, is the concealment. It does not signify whether it aided or did not aid the escape: it is indeed, of so little importance, that even if the convict had not been ultimately able to save himself, had he been retaken in the very place which served as his asylum, the man who had procured it for him would have been not the less guilty.

In one word, concealment is a distinct offence from that of escape; and to establish this point of criminal law unanswerably, it is sufficient to compare the enactments of the law on the two subjects.

In the offence of escape, all who co-operated in it are punished; there is no distinction, except in the penalties, for he who is placed as the keeper is more guilty than him who is not; beyond this the quality of the person is no farther regarded; and though public opinion may revolt at it, and humanity shed a tear, a son is not at liberty, legally speaking, to aid his father, nor a wife her husband, in breaking prison; and if Madame Lavalette has not been brought to trial, it was because, notwithstanding her ostentatious declarations, justice remained doubtful, and thought that it still perceived the influence of the marital authority in the act by which a wife assisted her husband.

Why, then, this severity of principle? The reason doubtless is, that the prison is a sacred and inviolable place; that those confined there belong no more to society but to justice, which detains them till they answer for their crimes. In the offence of concealment, neither does the law punish without distinction; it follows the dictates of nature; and pious exceptions are laid down for the father, the son, the spouse, the brother, and other relatives in the same degree. Here clemency stops, and justice commences, Hence, all who conceal a convict, with whom they are not connected by ties of blood, are culpable.— Bruce, Hutchinson, and Wilson will, therefore, be guilty, if they have concealed Lavalette.

But it is necessary to establish the culpability; and I know not but it may be intended to contest with the public accuser the right of searching for and producing the proofs —a circumstance very astonishing indeed; but the whole affair has its singularities. It would appear that, in default of questions of fact or of law, it presents problems to be resolved. Whence arises this? It proceeds from its being endeavoured to transform a judicial discussion into a political one; it proceeds from this, that the accused place themselves in the falsest position, imagining that they are accused of a system, when they are only accused, and have only to defend themselves on a fact. However, the *instruction* of the process must not be confounded with the accusation. The *instruction* may extend to a thousand facts; the accusation is confined to one. The *instruction* is the inquiry; it reaches every thing, both facts inculpatory and exculpatory—to facts and to circumstances, for it is by them that facts are characterised, that they become culpable or innocent, that they constitute a crime or an offence, or that they do not constitute an offence.

What then happened on this business? There have been the concealment and escape of Lavalette. Justice makes her inquiries; at first, those only are found who were implicated in the escape from prison; and when it is about to terminate its inquiries, a ray of unexpected light is thrown on the mystery of the concealment: other men and other projects are discovered. Those engaged in the escape from prison meant nothing but to save Lavalette: those engaged in his concealment, by saving Lavalette, wished, or at least appear to have wished, to excite to sedition or to revolt; and to excite any kind of disorder, provided only it was disorder.

But the plan was foolish! Doubtless it was: still, however, we must examine it. We must see by what hands the apple of discord was to be thrown amongst us; and the correspondence teaches us, that some foreigners were seriously employed on the happiness of France, that they were at work upon it, and that they would derive great joy from their success ! It is true, however, that they are in need of assistance, and that we shall take good care to give them none, How, then, were they to make us happy in spite of ourselves ? How, Gentlemen ? Why, as was done in 1793, The correspondents did not know any better means apparently, because there are no other. Thus an appeal was to be made to the friends of liberty, who were to put themselves in motion ; there were to be movements in the provinces ; and, above all, a good means of agitation would be the persecution of the Protestants, real or pretended ! Oh ! excellent ! This is an idea which catches like wildfire, which spreads like contagion in general, (and mark this) which engenders a spirit of mortal hatred and contempt for the new dynasty.

It is clear that, if the people were so totally misled, the revolution would be complete ; and it is for this very reason that revolution is impossible. Edward Wilson, at London, judged better of the state of France than his brother did at Paris. He began to distrust his predictions, and wait for facts. He remarks, *that if the French nation generally were strongly disinclined to the Bourbons, proofs of this would be daily manifested.* And he adds this observation : *It so happens that there is no military force in the provinces, and yet the provinces are tranquil.* On this subject he becomes inflamed, and says that if it is wished to overturn the existing order of things, *the fire must be constantly kept, and constantly visible, like a beacon of alarm in France and in foreign countries.*

May God avert this from us and from foreign countries also! We have all of us seen the sinister planet, portentous of storms ; the storm is passed, and new signs announce to us that the earth is pacified. Yes, we are at peace among ourselves, and we will be so with others. The nations are at peace, with the single exception of some turbulent men, to whom *peace is war*, as our old Montaigne has observed. Very well, let them remain in war, its theatre shall not be extended ; but let them not imagine in their foolish thoughts that they will agitate France ; if their *beacon of alarm* is perceived, we shall only hasten to extinguish it, as we run to put out a fire.

Attend to these words :—There is *no military force* in the provinces, and the provinces are *tranquil.* Yes, they are so, though they suffer ; but they arm themselves with fortitude against their misfortune, and turn their eyes towards that legitimate King whom Providence has restored to us ; for he has brought with him both the paternal virtues which make Kings cherished, and the ancient principles on which at all times the welfare of France has reposed. He is come to give stability to that country which revolutions had shaken —to unite, to repair, to absorb, by his inexhaustible goodness, those fratricidal hatreds which party-spirit had excited among Frenchmen. He has come ! and already Hope has occupied the place of reality, we already, by anticipation, emerge from our calamities, and the means of prosperity which belong to France are incontestibly fixed. She was weak for a moment, because she was misled and divided. Wisdom and union will restore to her strength, and the illustrious rank which she can never lose among the nations. This is a point demonstrated to all just-thinking men, but it is one also which never can be appreciated—which cannot be comprehended by the *Bruces* and the *Wilsons* of England.

In fine, the correspondence is a tissue of visions, calculated, indeed, to throw a light upon, though they do not change the nature of the offence. And if it be asked why justice has adverted to them at all, it may be fairly replied, that she is entitled to do so for her own information. I shall now, however confine myself to the terms of the indictment ; and shall investigate whether the three prisoners were accomplices in the concealment of Lavalette. As to the fact of the discovery of the documents, all that justice knows of them is, that she has received them as proofs. Should the prisoner Wilson renew his complaints on this head, should he (which I do not anticipate) attack the good faith of Government, I would say to him—Represent to your own mind the position in which you placed yourself ; reflect that you were, at least in intention, in a state of war ; the police had its eyes upon you as upon your fellow-prisoner Bruce ; the police of London would have done as much in a similar case ; there is no Government so simple as to respect the pretended rights of those who do not respect its repose.

Art. 248 of the Penal Code declares guilty those who have *concealed,* or caused to the *concealed.* Such are the terms of the law. The nature of the facts is such, that there is already a moral conviction, that those who concerted to get Lavalette out of France, also came to an understanding as to the mode of its accomplishment, the moment the escape from prison took place ; he who wills the end, wills the means. It is also equally certain, that Lavalette, issuing from an unknown retreat, had need of some place of depot, where he might be at the disposal of those who meant to carry him off. You have not heard it said that there was on their part any communication with the first asylum where Lavalette was secreted ; this was not necessary : it was sufficient that they provided for him an intermediate asylum ; and, by his passing the night there, that asylum became the place of concealment. This first position is incontestible.

There is a second observation which will not escape you. A person may conceal a man either at his own house, or that of another, according as he shall believe that he will in either way the better provide for his security ; and hence the law speaks of *concealing*, or *causing* to be concealed. He then, who furnishes the asylum, may be far from being the alone guilty person. He who procures it ; he who has made arrangements for procuring it ; in fine, the introducer who facilitates his entrance into it, are all evidently abettors, accomplices, and adherents in this species of crime.

What now happened ? For the accused Hutchinson the fact is material. Lavalette passed in his apartments in the rue Helder the night between the 7th and the 8th of January last. Hutchinson knew well that Lavelette was condemned, and it was indeed his condemnation that excited the interest which he felt in his fortunes. Thus, with respect to him, all the conditions of the law are fulfilled, or rather all the prohibitions of the law are violated, and the accused stands convicted of the crime charged.

The prisoner Bruce is not in a situation that admits of greater doubt. It was to him that the first disclosure was made. He was the man who inspired a predilection into the condemned ; for he who declared himself so zealously in the affair of Marshal Ney, would naturally be expected to sympathise with the situation of Lavalette. Reliance was placed on him, therefore, before trial was made. You see how he prided himself in the action, how he claimed the first share in the inheritance of glory. *If any one is guilty, he is the man.* Nothing farther could be required to establish the crime of which he is guilty. He concealed likewise the condemned. The hour and the place of meeting were agreed upon with the rest. In consequence, he is found with Hutchinson on the evening of Sunday; he there receives Lavalette. It is he who receives him principally, for at the appointed hour he descends to meet Lavalette; he conducts him from the street door to the apartment which was appointed for him, and into it he leads the condemned with his own hand, for in such a delicate matter he must do every thing himself to make sure of success. No question is asked of the porter, whom they saw—they do not address themselves to a servant. It is necessary that an official usher should attend to introduce the stranger as the friend of the family. If such conduct does not establish the offence of concealment charged on the prisoners, let it be declared where a more marked co-operation could be found.

As for the accused Wilson, he will pretend, perhaps, that he is not included in the same proof of guilt; for in strictness he can say—" I happened accidentally to be with my friend Hutchinson; I went to his lodgings to enjoy my share of a bowl of punch, and I saw M. Lavalette arrive. The meeting was accidental, and shall I be liable to punishment for having merely seen Lavalette?"

This language, if it came from the lips of a man who had no other communications with Lavalette, might be conclusive. As matters are at present, it signifies nothing. There is here a compact between three men to forward the escape of M. Lavalette, and of course, to conceal his person previous to his escape. To effect the project of saving him without knowing where to find him, would amount to an absurdity that the accused Englishmen cannot be supposed capable of entertaining for a moment. If, instead of a common co-operation, there had been merely individual acts—if every one had carried on his projects apart from the rest, it might be conjectured that who saw part would not be able to see the whole, and that his operations, being without any certain end, could not succeed. But, in truth, this is not the fact. It is impossible for Wilson, who was on the morning of the 8th at the gate of the house in the Rue de Helder, for the purpose of receiving Lavalette, to say that he did not know his retreat, and still farther to declare that he had not contributed to supply him with one. Do we not here speak of one and the same transaction connected between them? To conceal Lavalette, and lead him off, the three coadjutors, therefore, must necessarily have concurred in a plan arranged for the whole transaction. I might ask if the offence of concealment *(le recele)* does not consist entirely in the act of affording an asylum ; if to disguise a man be not likewise one of the means of concealing him, of secreting him from the pursuit of justice ; if he who ordered his measure to be taken, who furnished the uniform of an English officer, he who, to use an expression of his own, dressed him on the road *(fait le toilette en route)*, by cutting off some white hairs which appeared from below his *coiffure ;* if all these are not indiscriminately guilty of having disguised, concealed, and protected (recele) Lavalette ? But on this point I shall not enter into controversy, it will be terminated in another way. An asylum at Paris was not enough, another was necessary on the road—they stopped at Compiegne. At this time Wilson, who accompanied the traveller, who had given orders that the carriage should arrive at Compiegne at such an hour, and should stop at such a house, was not a stranger to the choice of his lodging ; it was pre-engaged before their arrival ; they concealed in it Lavalette. He himself has told us why the place was appropriate—how retired, how solitary it was, and how little there he had to encounter the gaze of the curious and inquisitive. I must add, that there, contrary to the dictates of justice, Wilson concealed *(receloit)* Lavalette.

The Learned Counsel entered into a variety of further arguments, which want of room prevents us from inserting, and concluded as follows : " I trust that I have sufficiently developed the facts, and I shall conclude by calling your attention to the circumstances which aggravate them. I speak not of the intention, although the intention constitutes the essence of the offence, and though in this case the intention was truly perverse and detestable ; I speak not to you of the material circumstance of the offence generally ; the facts of escape and cocealment are in themselves timid acts—they are effected by prudence and stratagem ; he who flies, or who conceals himself has no wish to brave any one ; but here the final escape was conducted with arms, and both he who fled, and those who accompanied him, were determined to employ force, if necessary. I pass over the circumstances of the led horses, in order that the flight might be more rapid, in case of obstacles—this was in the nature of the transaction, in the necessity of their situation—but their possession of arms ! and against whom were they to be used ?—against the public agents of French authority—against those who are charged with its orders—

against all those indiscriminately to whom the superintendence and defence of public order have been intrusted. Here, then, the offence partook of the initiative of an attack on the State; and in this point of view, which it is impossible to disjoin, it acquires all the gravity of which it is perceptible. It has, then, called for the warmest reprobation, the strongest repression, and the utmost extent of the punishment which the law provides for similar offences."

WEDNESDAY, APRIL 24.

At half-past ten the Sitting was opened.

M. *Conflans was first heard in defence of his client Guerin.*

M. Dupin then spoke as follows, in behalf of the three Englishmen:—Gentlemen—On the same Bench where usually appear only obscure criminals, you see to-day three Gentlemen, whom their noble birth, the elevation of their sentiments, and their honourable character, would, it must have been presumed, have for ever preserved them from such a misfortune; but such is the effect of prejudice, which builds on appearances, which always goes beyond the truth, and which, though created with inconceivable facility, it requires efforts to destroy. My clients have experienced this to their great disadvantage: a sort of public indignation was at first excited against them—marked them out as a thing less, it was said, than the overthrow of the political system of all the States of Europe. However, they succeeded in justifying themselves on this head: their defence was heard, and, above all, felt. Thanks be given to justice, and to the wisdom of the Chamber of Accusation.

If thus their lives ceased to be threatened, their defence therefore, has not solely for its object to spare them an imprisonment more or less long—this is the least of their concern; but what they wish before all and above all, is, to preserve for themselves, for their families, for the nation more or less compromised, a consideration so justly acquired.

Their journey would have been still a mystery, had not Wilson committed the imprudence of intrusting the secret of it to paper; and even this imprudence would have led to no discovery, if the letter had reached the noble Lord to whom it was addressed, under the respectable cover of the English Ambassador. But the journals have told us of the treachery of a domestic of Wilson; and the letter having thus reached the hands of the French police, nothing more was requisite as a ground for their arrest. The forms in which they were proceeded against excited their protest, because they were opposite to their own laws, their modes, and their constitutional ideas. It was thus that Wilson, who refused to reply to the interrogatories, having been placed in secret custody, appealed to the habeas corpus law, being unable to conceive that he was bound to criminate himself.—This resistance did not originate in a contumacious spirit, but solely in ignorance of our laws. But the moment he had communicated with his Ambassador, what frankness, what good faith, in all that was personal to himself! and his two friends acted a similar part. Their interrogatories amply proved that their memory was not framed to betray confidence and friendship.

Here the Advocate retraced the proceedings in the course of the criminal inquiry which had at first for its object merely the escape of Lavalette, but to which was afterwards attached an imaginary conspiracy against all Europe. He contended that the arret of the Chamber of Accusation having set aside this pretended conspiracy, it ought not to have been reproduced either in the indictment or in the speeches of Counsel. His clients could not be considered as provoking the discussion, since they were compelled to defend themselves. Here, said M. Dupin, my task is a difficult one; if I defend my clients with energy, I may, perhaps, incur the charge of being a bad citizen; if I display weakness, I may be accused of basely deserting my clients—*Incedo per ignes.* But, for the sake of the strangers who listen to us, for the honour of our own nation, it should be known that an Englishman will find here as zealous defenders as he could have found in his own country.

(Here some expressions of applause having proceeded from a remote part of the Hall, the President ordered silence, remarking—" people applaud at a Theatre—they listen in a Court of justice.")

M. Dupin proceeded to remark on some serious errors which had crept into the translation of Wilson's letters.

The President stated to M. Dupin that he would call the interpreter, because he was willing that the defence of the prisoners should have all possible latitude.

After some explanations about an unimportant part of one of the letters, Sir R. Wilson said—We are satisfied as to the benevolent dispositions of the Court; but there are two sorts of tribunals—the one of justice and the other of public opinion; it is to the latter, especially, that we wish to justify ourselves.

The President—Wilson, there is in France only one sort of tribunal—that which tries in the name of the King.

M. Dupin pointed out several passages mistaken in his client's correspondence; and among others, that in which he speaks of a great movement which must be caused, and which only related to a motion to be announced to the Parliament of England. Relative to the passage which spoke of the discontent of the Protestants, M. Dupin observed, that the brother of the accused, in one of whose letters was to be found the passage noted, merely indicated the persecution, real or imaginary, of the Protestants, as one of the causes of discontent which existed against the royal government.

The Foreman of the Jury—You give a contradiction.

M. Dupin—Of the same extent as the allegation against me.

The Foreman—Then the whole of the letters should be read. (It was thought that this was unnecessary.)

The President—In virtue of my discretionary power, I invite the translator, who has already translated these papers, to fix, in conjunction with the interpreter, Mr. John Roberts, the meaning of the passages marked by M. Dupin.

The translator, after being sworn, expressed his fear that the operation would take up much time, because M. Wilson's writing was very difficult to read.

Sir R. Wilson then took his brother's letter of the 8th of January, and read to the interpreters the passage of which they had to fix the meaning. He observed to the Court, that the letter should not be read entire, because it contained some improper (peu convenables) expressions.

The interpreter then commenced his translation, but was interrupted by the Court.

The Advocate-General—I abandon to the prisoners all the deductions which they may draw from this correspondence. They may give the most favourable interpretation to all the passages indicated in the act of accusation, in order to justify themselves from the intention which we have ascribed to them.

M. Dupin—After such a concession, I confine myself to the remark, that the letter, in which is the passage marked, is a recital and not a counsel. Besides, it would be merely the opinion of the brother of his client, and nothing could be deduced from it against the latter.

" The public funds are falling. Bavaria and Austria are in arms." This was another of the passages for which Wilson's correspondence was reproached. This, however, was merely the repetition of Newspaper reports.

" He wished that the debates of the Parliament of England could be published in France. " What was this but a wish proceeding from the nationality of an Englishman, who thinks that sounder political doctrine was not to be found elsewhere than in his Parliament? Besides, the French Police could prevent the introduction of the debates of the British Parliament, as soon as it might be thought dangerous.

It was also charged " that he transmitted prognostics of popular commotions." But let us advert to circumstances which the wisdom of the King has already removed from our immediate recollection; it was only a few months ago that agitators endeavoured to excite disturbances amongst us; and if Wilson was deceived on this point, he can only be reproached with having listened with too much facility to popular rumours.

" Wilson," it was also said, " thought proper to characterise several of our political events from his interpretation of the capitulation of Paris." Admitting this to be an error on his part, it was an error which originated in a feeling that attached the greatest importance to every thing connected with his country.

In a word, it is against acts, and not opinions, that we must here make war. True or false, these opinions belonged to the accused alone ; he was responsible for them to no one, particularly if he gave them no publicity, and he is an Englishman, to whom on this head the Constitution of his Country accords entire liberty.

This indefinite liberty of expressing opinions is balanced in England by the tendency of Ministers to enlarge their power ; and this liberty, which has been represented under the falsest colours, is very far from that unbridled license which was amongst us, the cause of so many calamities and so many crimes.

Think not, however, Gentlemen, that, in speaking thus, I place the English above us: for we also have both our liberty and our constitutional principles ; and by the freedom with which I defend my clients, they may judge that a subject of the King of France is as free as themselves.

It is time, however, Gentlemen, that I should make you acquainted, by his actions, with him whom it has been endeavoured to devote to public hatred, by describing him as an enemy of public order, and of the repose of nations. It is time to explain to you these hieroglyphics of honour which he wears on his breast. He is decorated with the Orders of the Red Eagle of St. Anne, of St. George, of Maria Theresa, of the Tower and Sword, of the Crescent, and of several others ; because he has served with distinction in Flanders, Holland, Ireland, at the Helder, in Egypt, Poland, Portugal, and Spain, in Russia, Prussia, Germany, and Italy ; because he has been charged with important missions at Constantinople, St. Petersburgh, &c.

He had already distinguished himself ; when scarcely 21, he went to serve in Egypt: uniting his arms to those of the Mussulmans, he obtained by his merits the order of the crescent from the Grand Seignor ; and, joining literary to military merit, he became the first historian of that famous expedition, where the uncle of Hutchinson commanded in chief the English army.

Wilson went again to combat Bonaparte in Spain, where he powerfully contributed to arrest his progress by himself raising that Portuguese legion which had so great an influence on the fate of the peninsula.

H

It was in this war he became acquainted with Marshal Ney: he fears not to avow that he was conquered by him, but in his defeat he had reason for praising the generosity of the conqueror; and hence the origin of that interest which from ignorance of its deriving its source from a just gratitude, has been ascribed to political considerations.

At Moscow Bonaparte had still Wilson opposed to him. In his bulletins he complains bitterly of that English commissary: this is in other words, to attest the services which Wilson performed in that campaign.

When Moreau received his mortal wound, Wilson was close by that General, and was the first to raise him and afford him succour.

In fine, and to finish the picture, the eldest of Wilson's sons is a midshipman on board of the Northumberland, that vessel which conveyed Bonaparte to St. Helena.——

I now ask you gentlemen, whether General Wilson be an enemy of the good cause—whether he is a Bonapartist? for that is the epithet with which it has been sought to tarnish his character.

Wilson has performed signal services to all the sovereigns of Europe; he has had the happiness to be so also, in more than one instance, useful to his Majesty Louis XVIII.—to that sovereign whose memory is strong enough to retain the smallest services.—

Here M. Dupin read the five following letters:—

GENERAL WILSON—When I decorated you before the troops with my military order of St. George of the 3d class, I did justice to the indefatigable zeal which, during the whole campaign, constantly fixed you at the advanced posts; to the brilliant valour and devotedness of which I was witness at the battle of Bautzen, and to so many other proofs of intrepidity attested by all the brave men of the combined armies, it is gratifying to me now to repeat to you in writing the testimonies to which you have so marked a title, and to assure you of my sentiments.

(Signed)   ALEXANDER.

Toeplitz, 27th Sept. 1813.

GEN. WILSON.—At the moment when you are about to quit the armies, where I have had such frequent opportunities to do justice to your zeal and most brilliant valour, in order to follow another destination, I have resolved to give you a new proof of my satisfaction by decorating you with my order of St. Ann of the first class. You will find herewith enclosed its decorations. The brave men, by whose side you have so often fought, will regret you. For myself, I shall always recollect your courage and your indefatigable activity; and should events again bring you back to your old brothers in arms, I shall see you with pleasure. I pray God, &c.

(Signed)   ALEXANDER.

Friburg, Dec. 24, 1813.

GENERAL—I feel gratified by the sentiments which you express to me in your letter of the 1st of January. In justice to the zeal you have displayed in the good cause, and particularly to your attachment to my person, I shall feel a pleasure in proving to you, on every occasion the interest which I feel for you.

(Signed)   FREDERICK WILLIAM.

Bar-sur-Seine, Feb. 7, 1814.

GENERAL—The Emperor having informed me that you have lost the cross of the order of Maria Theresa in consequence of a conduct as brilliant as fine, which in itself would have merited that distinction, has charged me, as chancellor of the order, to transmit to you a fresh decoration, to which you daily acquire new claims. Conservator of this fine institution, I feel personally interested in seeing worn, by men of your merit, a mark of valour on which they do not shed less lustre than they receive from it.

(Signed)   Prince METTERNICH.

Toeplitz, Sept. 24, 1813.

GENERAL—I feel particular satisfaction in being able to announce to you, that his Majesty the Emperor, wishing to give you a special mark of the esteem with which you have inspired him, both by the services you have performed as a soldier, and by the faithful conduct which has distinguished you during your residence at head quarters, which his Imperial Majesty sees you quit with regret, has resolved to grant you the cross of commander of his order of Maria Theresa.

My sentiments are shared by an army which has been witness to your brilliant conduct, and by all my compatriots who have been in a situation which enabled them to appreciate the qualities of your heart.

(Signed)   Prince METTERNICH.

Fribourgh, Jan. 4, 1814.

M. Dupin next detailed some traits of Sir R. T. Wilson's humanity.

In 1808, he found a great number of French prisoners in Spain. The son of the Duke of Feltre, the nephew of Prince Talleyrand, owed to him their safety in the Russian campaign : it was Wilson also who saved the celebrated French physician Desgenetts, and who gave him succours for the French prisoners.

Well! Wilson, distinguished by so many traits of beneficence; Bruce, the nephew of the celebrated traveller, and who has travelled himself in order to enrich science with his observations ; and Hutchinson, still too young to enable me to speak to you of his life, but who came among us by the paths of honour—all three are deprived of their liberty, and appear before you as prisoners for an act of generosity, which the very Arabs of the Desert would have pronounced worthy of the finest recompence.

Having now reached the principal point in the case, I reduce it to two very simple propositions ; 1st, There was here no act of complicity between the accused Englishmen and the culprit ;

2d, The fact imputed to them cannot be considered as a crime, nor as offence.

Taking his ground on article 60th of our code, M. Dupin showed that complicity supposes direct and necessary relations between the chief culprit and him who is marked as accomplice ; and that, in this case, not the least connection could be indicated between the Englishmen and any other persons accused.

The means furnished to Lavalette for quiting France could not constitute complicity in the offence of escape (evasion), because the escape was then consummated. The very meaning of the word indicated this, for we found in the dictionary of the academy the following phrase, which appeared completely in point : he skilfully got out of prison, and after his escape (evasion) he retired to a place of safety.

If on the 8th January, the day when Lavalette was executed in effigy, any one had thought proper to demand a delay of that execution, on the ground that the escape was still not consummated, he would not have failed to have been considered as a madman or a fool.

Proceeding to the 2d proposition, M. Dupin laid it down that there could be no concealment, unless where there was an intention to secrete or conceal ; but such intention could not be supposed in this case, since the stay for a few hours of the convict Lavalette at Hutchinson's lodgings had solely for its object to facilitate his departure. Hutchinson, by military quarters, could not besides give an asylum to any one at his house ; he might receive, every minute, an order to depart, and in this view a concealment (recele) at his house was impossible.

Besides, added he, the acknowledgment of Hutchinson is the only proof existing on the trial of the short stay which Lavalette made with him ; this confession must, therefore, be taken simply as it stands ; he has declared, however, he was urged by an anonymous letter to procure Lavalette the means of departure from Paris, and not to conceal him. The passports demanded, and the cabriolet furnished by Bruce, sufficiently indicated, also that the object was the departure of the convict, and his concealment.

Our criminal laws forbid the procuring of liberty to him who is detained in prison, or intrusted to an escort ; but Lavalette had recovered his state of natural liberty, when the three Englishmen lent him their aid. They enabled him to get out of Paris—of France—but not out of prison.

It was a pure sentiment of humanity which, in this affair, directed the conduct of Bruce and of Wilson ; and why were we not to believe that a man might interest himself for another who was unknown to him? Towards a relative, a friend, this sentiment would be a duty : towards a stranger, it was merely a noble movement of the soul.

At Athens, a young man was capitally condemned for having

killed a pigeon, which had taken refuge in his bosom, because it was thought that he who was without pity must be always a bad citizen: and among us, in the 19th century, shall a man be condemned for having saved another man?

My clients are strangers, are Englishmen; and this is precisely the reason why you owe to them all your justice, as I owe to them all my zeal. You will thus verify that fine thought of a celebrated Chancellor of France—" Strangers are sacred persons with us, when they invoke the justice of the King."

This Speech being closed, the President asked of Bruce whether he passed the night of the 7th of January at Hutchinson's apartments?

Bruce—No, Sir, I retired at midnight.

The President.—General Wilson, however, writes in his letter, that, when at night there was a knocking at the door, you exclaimed, " We are discovered."

Wilson—I beg pardon of the President, but the following are the words of my letter—" M. Lavalette then himself exclaimed, we are discovered."

The President.—Sir R. T. Wilson, did you write that you were armed and prepared to defend yourselves?

Wilson—Mr. President, as I am anxious that my friends and all those who are present at this trial should believe me incapable of altering the truth, I will read to you the passage from my letter, relative to the fact as to which you interrogate me:—

" We were prepared for resistance; but we placed much more dependence on our presence of mind."

The proceedings having closed, Sir R. Wilson rose, and, with a dignified assurance, delivered a speech of which the following is the substance:—

" Monsieur Le President,

" You did me too much honour in the proceeding of the day before yesterday, by saying that I had a profound knowledge of the French language. Unfortunately I am but little familiarised in it: I even speak it very badly. I must therefore beg, and hope to obtain your indulgence.

" I might begin by thanking the Court for the full liberty they have given our Advocate, and the justice we have experienced during the proceedings. Being not sufficiently acquainted with the code of your laws, the principles and forms of which are essentially different from those of England, we have entrusted our defence entirely to our Advocate, and we owe him all our gratitude, not only for the efforts of his talents, and that eloquence which he knows how to display on all occasions, but also for the generous zeal which he has unceasingly manifested in our cause.

" There are yet explanations which remain for me to give, and

H 2

which I intend to do with all the respect that I owe to authority, and to the majesty of justice.

" Gentlemen, you are not ignorant that a much heavier accusation has fallen on our heads.

" Threatened by this attack, directed against our life and honour, we have sought our safety neither in the policy of cabinets nor in clemency.

" Trusting in our innocence, we have demanded from no government any thing but the protection of an impartial judgment, and we [have found our Ægis in the wisdom and justice of the Chamber of Accusation.

" Nevertheless, notwithstanding the decision of that Chamber, the prosecutors have persisted in inserting in the act of Accusation, a collection of facts foreign to the crime of which we are now accused ; and while they have designated me as the enemy of all governments, on account of observations intended for the most sacred confidence, they have loaded me, in the face of Europe, with the most outrageous and calumnious expressions.

" Born in a free country, educated with the right of thinking freely on all subjects, and of communicating my thoughts, whether by speech or writing, I have made use of this right.

" Animated by love for justice, humanity and liberty (not revolutionary liberty, but that liberty on which the social order of my country is founded, and which we cherish as the vivifying principle of our happiness and our power), I have always expressed myself in my correspondence with the ardour that these sentiments inspire in me.

" These may no doubt be found in this correspondence, news, anecdotes, predictions which have not been verified. Knowing that they would never be made public by those to whom my letters were addressed, I communicated them without much consideration, but there is not one opinion of mine on the morality of politics that I am not proud to avow and ready to defend.

" It is true, that I imagined I saw on the political horison of Europe, storms ready to break out again, and lightning ready to burst forth ; I thought I saw this fair France still suffering, and still removed from the happiness which, with all my soul I wish her to possess ; but I have only traced the foundation on which this belief was founded.

" Religion : yes, Gentlemen, my political Religion hinders me from interfering in the internal concerns of other nations. I pity their misery ; I wish them prosperity ; I would wish to see, as my Advocate says, every man free and every state independent, but I have never formed these wishes as a Conspirator.—Devoted to honour and the Constitution of my country, I oppose and will always oppose, every system, every act which, according to my opinion wounds them, or even threatens them; but I march under the unfolded banner of that same Constitution, and my colours are neither the dagger nor poision, but the rights and laws of my country.

" Gentlemen, do not think it a crime for an Englishman to watch over the projects, and to set himself up as a judge over the acts of his Government. The liberty and the reputation of his country is his patrimony; he cannot cease to be their guardian, without betraying what he owes to his ancestors, to his fellow-citizens, and to posterity.

" Arbitrary governments demand a blind devotion from their subjects: but a constitutional State requires from all classes of its citizens the most jealous vigilance over the Government itself. Nature, honour, and religion add to the obligation; and the exercise of this duty is the proud prerogative of a free man; and this is a truth which you will not doubt, when you shall have lived longer under your constitutional regime.

" My principles have been denounced as dreadful; but the people will hardly be persuaded, that principles which announce an attachment to good faith, clemency, patriotism, and philanthropy, are principles which arise from a criminal source; but it is from intercepted letters that proofs of criminality have been endeavoured to be derived against me. The violation of correspondence is a crime: thus it will have been by the id of a crime that it has been wished to prove against me a correctional offence. I do not dwell upon this point; but I thought it my duty to point out this circumstance to the meditation of the Jury.

" But who has given publicity to my thoughts?—Who are they who have got possession, and by what means have they got possession of a correspondence addressed only to my friends and countrymen—addressed only to the eyes of a brother, and of a personage whose name bears with it a guarantee of all that is most illustrious and most loyal in a nation of which he has constantly been one of the most enlightened and most zealous supporters?

" The Procureur of the King has seemed not to wish that I should speak of these means; but as he wishes to take advantage of the fortuitous trait of a crime, which by the French legislature is punished by afflictive and infamous penalties, and to present it as the proof, and the only proof, which there is of a crime purely correctional, I have been obliged to raise the question, and I hope the jury will give it all the attention it deserves.

" I will not enter into other details, since our Advocate has done us justice so nobly, and vindicated the honour of my brother connected not only with the honour of his family, but that of the nation.

" As to the charge of having conducted M. Lavalette out of the French territory, I will not detain you long. The fact is acknowledged, I have only to detain you as to the motives. It is true that the character of M. Lavalette, with whom otherwise I had no particular connection, had inspired me with an interest which I saw was felt by all classes of society in France.

" The painful sacrifices, the interesting devotedness, and the boldness so wisely calculated, of Madame Lavalette, had singularly increased that interest; and where is the man—where is the man who could have seen without pain and regret the glory and happiness of this virtuous and for ever illustrious woman, end in misery and desolation?

" It is true also that I looked on M. Lavalette as a man condemned in a revolutionary time for a crime purely political; and who having also surrendered himself voluntarily, confiding in his innocence, and the presumed validity of treaties made with the Allied Powers, deserved all our interest; but I declare that these powerful reflections have had a very secondary influence in my determination.

" The appeal made to our humanity, to our personal character, and our national generosity, the responsibility cast on us, of deciding suddenly on the safety or death of an unfortunate man, and, above all, of an unfortunate stranger:—this appeal was imperative, and did not permit us to calculate his other titles to our benevolence.

" At the voice of this appeal, we should have done as much for a person unknown, or an enemy fallen into misfortune; perhaps we have been defective in prudence; but we prefer, and we rejoice at this moment, at having yielded to the feelings of our hearts.

" And these same men who have calumniated us without knowing either the motives or details of our conduct—these same men I say, would have been the first to denounce us as cowards without honour and without patriotism, if by our refusal to save M. Lavalette we had abandoned him to certain death.

" Our friends and countrymen would have joined their reproaches to those of our enemies, and thus degraded by the just contempt of the world, consumed by our own shame, and deserving the death with which we were afterwards threatened, we should have drawn out an odious and tarnished existence.

" Gentlemen, I abandon myself with confidence to the generous feelings of a jury purely French. If in your minds you think that we have offended the laws of your country, and that we owe it a satisfaction, we shall have at least the consolation of knowing that we have not offended the laws of nature, and that we have performed the duties of humanity."

This speech, pronounced in a firm and decent tone, made a lively impression on the public; and notwithstanding the respect and reserve which should be preserved in Court, applauses were heard throughout almost all the Hall.

Hutchinson declared that he had nothing to add to the speech of his Counsel.

M. the President having asked M. Bruce if he had any thing to add to his defence, Bruce spoke as follows:—

"I appear before a Court of justice, on an accusation of having contributed to the escape of Lavalette; if it is a crime to have saved the life of a man, I avow that I am guilty.

"I did not wish to derive any vanity from what I have been able to do; an appeal was made to my humanity, and my honour imposed on me the obligation of answering it. If the accusation had been confined to the affair of Lavalette, I should have but few words to say to you; but I have been accused of having conspired against the political system of Europe, of having excited the inhabitants of France to take arms against the authority of the King. It is true that this charge, absurd, ridiculous, destitute of all foundation, and which has excited equal astonishment and indignation throughout Europe, has been rejected by the wisdom of the Chamber of Accusation. But although this accusation has been rejected, the motives on which it was founded still subsist. The Procureur-General, in his act of accusation, has allowed himself to say—

M. the President.—Accused, you speak French with very great facility; in speaking, therefore, of a Magistrate, and of so respectable a Magistrate, measure your expressions.

"M. Bruce continued.—The Procureur-General said, that I am one of those persons who are imbued with anti-social doctrines; that I am an enemy, from principle, of all order and government —an enemy, from principle, of all Kings, of justice, and of humanity; and the friend of the factious in all countries. These, it must be confessed, are grave accusations; but the explanation which I am going to give of my principles will be a conclusive answer to these calumnious allegations.

"I shall not enter into metaphysical abstractions on the rights of man, nor into digressions on politics; I will confine myself to a description of the principles which have always directed my political actions.

"I was born an Englishman, I love with enthusiasm the constitution of my country—that is to say, the constitution as established by our glorious revolution of 1688. It was then that was formed that most beautiful system of Government which excites so universal an admiration; which serves as a model to other nations, which makes our country called, by distinction, the classic land of liberty, which earned for us the deserved eulogium of the philosopher Montesquieu, who is the patrimony not only of France, but of all the world, and who said of us—"The English are the only people in the world who know how to make use of their religion, their laws, and their commerce." From the revolution of 1688 may be dated the prosperity, the greatness, and the liberty of England.

"I am bound to say, that if these principles, which are mine, and which are those of the constitution of my country, are subversive of all idea of order and good government, and make me the enemy of Kings, of justice, and of humanity. I am then the most guilty of men, and my accuser is in the right.

"But if, on the contrary, these are the principles which procured for us our protecting laws, which secure to us our persons, our properties, and our religion, which have made of a people little favoured by nature or by fortune the most happy, the best governed and most flourishing nation of Europe, I have a right to conclude that the accusation is nothing but a reviling calumny. Yes; such are the principles of that Wilson and of that Bruce, of whom the Advocate-General spoke in so indecorous a manner. I inherited them from my ancestors—I shall carry them to my grave.

"As to the affair of M. de Lavalette, politics had nothing to do with it; I was moved only by the sentiments of humanity. You have seen, from my interrogatory that I was hardly acquainted with him. It is true, that the goodness of his character, the amiability of his disposition, and the sweetness of his manners, had inspired me with a greater interest than is usually felt for a person whom one has seen so little. I was, never at his house—he had never been at mine; and it was here, where I appear as an accused person, that I had the honour of seeing, for the first time, that virtuous and interesting wife, and been enabled to pay her the homage of my devoted and respectful admiration.

"It has been demonstrated to you, that there was no connexion between us and the other persons accused. I respected the chains and gates of the house of justice. I did not go like Don Quixote, in quest of adventures but an unfortunate man comes and asks my protection; he shows a confidence in my character; he puts his life into my hands; he appeals to my humanity! What would have been said of me, if I had denounced him to the police? I should then have deserved that death with which I have since been threatened. What do I say? What would have been thought of me, if I had refused to protect him? I should have been looked upon as a poltroon, as a man without principle, without honour, without courage, without generosity; I should have deserved the contempt of all good men.

"But, Gentlemen, there were other considerations which decided me. There was something romantic in the story of Lavalette. His miraculous escape from prison, that cruel uncertainty between death and life in which he so long remained—the noble devotedness of his wife, that French Alcestis—her heroic action, which will live in history—all struck my imagination, and excited in my heart an interest so lively, that I could not resist its impulse ; besides, as one La Fontaine says, who in his simplicity has said every thing :—

"Dans ce monde il se faut l'un l'autre secourir ;
"Il se faut entr'aider : c'est la loi de nature."

"Gentlemen, I am yet young, but I have travelled a great deal ; I have seen many countries, and have examined, with all the attention of which I am capable, the customs of the people. I have always observed, even among the most barbarous nations, among those who are almost in a state of primitive nature, that it is a sacred thing among them to succour those who have recourse to their protection ; it is a duty enjoined by their religion, by their laws, by their customs. A Bedouin of the desert, a Dreze of Mount Lebanon, would rather sacrifice his life than betray the man who had fled to him for an asylum : whatever be his country, whatever his crime, he sees only the duties of humanity and of hospitality : I, a civilized man, 'thought it my duty to imitate the virtues even of barbarians.

"And I cannot persuade myself that, among a people celebrated for their sensibility, their humanity, and their chivalrous character—which reckon among their Kings, a Henry IV. that model of a Prince—and would to God all Kings were like him—which reckon among their heroes a Bayard, the completest of all, without fear, without reproach, whose device was always to succour his distressed fellow-creatures—I cannot believe that, among such a people, an Englishman can be condemned for having saved the life of a Frenchman.

"Gentlemen, I have confessed to you, with all frankness and honour, the whole truth with respect to the part I took in the escape of M. Lavalette ; and, notwithstanding the respect which I entertain for the majesty of the laws—notwithstanding the respect which I owe to this Tribunal, I cannot be wanting in the respect which I owe to myself, by avowing that I feel the least repentance for what I have done.

"Gentlemen, I have now said all ; I leave you to decide upon my fate, and I implore nothing but justice."

This discourse pronounced with a strong foreign accent, and with a firm tone sustained throughout, produced like Wilson's, the liveliest impression ; and we heard several old advocates applaud equally the eloquence of the accused and of their defenders.

The President having asked of the prisoners, whether they had any thing further to add to their defence, proceeded to sum up the evidence. After a rapid exposition of the facts, M. de Seze stated to the Jury that he was fulfilling the functions of reporter, not those of Judge, and that it was his duty to present to them with equal care the accusation and the means of defence.

This Magistrate performed this difficult task with all the talent which characterizes him; and if the impartiality of his charge throughout proved the purity of his intentions, fine bursts of eloquence repeatedly betrayed the orator who made his debut at the bar under such brilliant auspices. He concluded by putting the the following questions to the Jury.

1. Is John Hely Hutchinson guilty of having, in the month of January last, concealed the said Lavalette, by giving him an asylum in the house where he lodged, knowing that the said Lavalette was condemned to capital punishment?

2. Is Michael Bruce guilty of having, in the month of January last, caused to be concealed the said Lavalette, in the house where Hutchinson lodged, knowing that the said Lavalette was condemned to capital punishment?

3. Is Robert Thomas Wilson guilty of having, in the month of January last, caused to be concealed the said Lavalette, in connection with the said Bruce and Hutchinson, knowing that the said Lavalette was condemned to capital punishment?

4. Is the said Wilson guilty of having, in the month of January last, caused to be concealed at Compeigne the said Lavalette, knowing that he was condemned to capital punishment?

At a quarter past four the Jury retired to deliberate, and the Court adjourned.

At five the Court resumed. The President of the Jury read as follows:—

With regard to the first question—Yes, the accused, Hutchinson, is guilty; to the 2d—Yes, the accused Bruce, is guilty; to the 3d—Yes, the accused, Wilson, is guilty; to the 4th—Yes, the accused, Wilson, is guilty.

In consequence, the Procureur-General having prayed the application of the punishment, the Court, after having deliberated, resumed its sitting, and by its arret condemned them to the lightest punishment sanctioned by law, viz. *three months imprisonment.*

FINIS.